MEMORIES OF CHILDHOOD

Childhood Memory #44—The Cellar: "Don't worry," said his sister sweetly, "I won't turn off the light…." by Elaine H. Spencer, Fort Collins, Colorado. 1988. 52″ x 43″. Cotton. *First Place Grand Prize Winner.* "Once, when I was a child, I did lock my brother in the basement and turn off the light," recalls Elaine Spencer, "but then, he did equally horrible things to me!" This clever and eyecatching quilt symbolizes all those deliciously fearful moments of childhood: after your parents turned off the bedroom light at night; a visit to the basement with the furnace looming threateningly in a corner; going out alone for the first time on a dark Halloween night—and the frightful yet delightful fantasies that accompanied them, but only in the imagination. The "monster" fabrics were chosen specifically because of their "ominous" appearance, the artist says. She calls finding fabric for a quilt "the thrill of the hunt" and notes that it is easy to get carried away—she now has more monster fabric than she can use! Some of the quilt fabrics are African, acquired when Elaine Spencer and her husband lived in Gambia and she spent "every extra minute in the market." She overdyed a few fabrics to create the right effect for the shadows and found out that dying has its unforeseen drawbacks. "My husband heated up some leftover liquid I had in a pan on the stove only to find out it was dye, not coffee! He is a much more cautious consumer of beverages in our kitchen now." The artist, a preschool and elementary schoolteacher for fourteen years, noted that children always love books with strong graphic qualities, and she tried to keep this in mind when creating this design. She spent six months working on and off on the quilt, and there were moments of discouragement. "Those stairs! I took one seam out twenty-two times and ended up throwing the piece across the room! Then the dog slept on the quilt, my husband sat on it, and I'll never use a marker pen again on a quilt!" During the course of its creation, the Spencers moved twice and built a new house, so "quilting became a refuge during that period." Elaine Spencer has been quilting since 1979 and is a member of the Colorado Quilters Council and three local groups: The Quilt Group, The Bag Ladies, and The Quilt Bats.

MEMORIES OF CHILDHOOD

Quilt Texts by
Jacqueline M. Atkins, Museum Editor

E. P. DUTTON   NEW YORK

In association with the
MUSEUM OF AMERICAN FOLK ART   NEW YORK

When Toys and I Were One by Jane Blair, Conshohocken, Pennsylvania. 1988. 54″ x 45″. Cotton, cotton polyester. *Second Place Grand Prize Winner.* Because "it has been a long time since I was a child, I had to put myself back into a child's world," Jane Blair said, who wrote a poem to help her focus on the design for this quilt. "The old horse was gray/I'm sure the boat was blue/My world was pretend/Each day was always fun/ When I was a child/And toys and I were one." From her experience as an elementary schoolteacher, she knew that children liked primary colors and strong graphics, so she decided that the basics of her design had to be toys, bright color, a good graphic element, and a sense of pretend. As she started drawing toys in rows, they seemed to come together to form the child, and there she had it—an exceptionally creative set of images for an extraordinary quilt. She does not write a poem for every quilt she makes, but it helped her to concentrate her thoughts in this case. The artist says that she always spends the most time on her design: first drawing it on graph paper, then adding color on a tracing paper overlay, and finally putting pieces up on her work wall before sewing them together so she can see how the fabrics will work together texturally. She does not think about the construction of the quilt when she designs, and this sometimes means that she must later become quite inventive in her sewing in order to solve structural problems. The rockers on the rocking horses are an example here—the points were extremely difficult to execute, but they worked! Jane Blair has made over one hundred quilts in her eighteen years of quilting. "My hands have to be busy; I have to do something, and this is it. It has everything I want in one thing." She has won awards in a number of contests, but if the project intrigues her she will do it whether or not she thinks she will win. Although she wasn't totally happy with this quilt ("I never am with any quilt I make"), her husband encouraged her to submit it anyway, and so she did. "After all," she says, "what did I have to lose?"

My Dolls by Hanne Wellendorph, Vemmelev, Denmark. 1988. 53″ x 44½″. Cotton, laces, linen. *Third Place Grand Prize Winner.* This quilt contains a wealth of childhood memories for the artist; the dolls shown in the cabinet are similar in type to those she had as a child, and the cabinet is one that belonged to her grandmother and is now housed in the artist's studio. Her twelve-year-old daughter picked out the fabric used for the dolls' hair ribbons and helped find others—most of which came from scraps of old dresses—for their clothes. Under the cabinet are tucked pieces of the artist's past: bits of old linen, a piece of her wedding dress, and dated cross-stitchery. "Every Danish girl learned how to do cross-stitches when I was young; cross-stitches are a big part of my childhood—they represent part of what I am today." The names of the artist's daughter, herself, and her mother—Petrine, Hanne, and Elyse—are quilted into the background of each shelf in the cabinet, and lively little figure drawings remembered from her childhood and her children's are quilted with *sashiko*-type stitching down the left and right sides of the cabinet. "Even though quilting is the hardest part, each stitch in the quilt makes it become more beautiful and more real." Although quilting (or patchwork, as it is often referred to in Denmark) is not a tradition in her country, Hanne Wellendorph has been an enthusiastic advocate, starting a national guild that now has five hundred members and a local club that includes two hundred quilters. She has also written four books on creative patchwork—one of which is in English—and has arranged for exhibitions of antique American quilts. In Denmark, she says, quilting is done mostly during the long dark winter months. "In summer, everyone wants to be outside in the sunshine. You have to be a fanatic in Denmark to quilt in the summertime." She says that her farm keeps her busy enough in the summer, so she exhibits, teaches quilting, and sews in the winter. She finds that she works mostly at night: "The quilting spirit comes to me at night; then the pencil making my designs just dances across the paper."

PREFACE

The program events for the first Great American Quilt Festival in 1986 had been so well received it was decided that they should be expanded for The Great American Quilt Festival 2. Special arrangements were made with the Fashion Institute of Technology to include events at their facility, and Karla Friedlich, program chairman of the Festival, and Janey Fire, director of photo services at the museum, developed innovative projects that extended significantly the traditional kinds of activities that usually accompany quilt shows.

A series of diverse lecture-symposia and large-scale workshops were designed. Each lecture-symposium featured a panel of three experts who focused on a specific quilting topic. The symposia were scheduled for the amphitheatre at the Fashion Institute of Technology, which seats 350 people. Samples of the work of each teacher were displayed. The format allowed each teacher time for a slide lecture and an intermission to be followed by a panel discussion with audience participation. Informal discussions in smaller groups and meetings with the teachers were also part of the planning.

The all-day and half-day workshops ranged from new trends in quilting to the refinement of traditional techniques and were structured for quilters at all levels of experience. Each workshop was planned to accomodate from 75 to 100 quilters, and each instructor was assisted by five knowledgeable aides. Each was planned to start with a slide-lecture introduction and then proceed to hands-on activity.

In addition to the lectures and classes developed by the museum, two showings of Fairfield Processing Corporation's Tenth Anniversary Wearable Art Fashion Show extravaganza were held at the Fashion Institute of Technology. Organized by Donna Wilder, this fashion show was exciting and outrageous and a great event.

The lecture-symposia and workshop leaders chosen for the festival represented every segment of the contemporary quilting world, and it is a pleasure to be able to make a special acknowledgement of the following artists/craftswomen who participated: Gerlinde Anderson-Harris, Virginia Avery, Ann Boyce, Barbara Brackman, Nancy Crow, Judy Dales, Luella Doss, Chris Wolf Edmonds, Deborah Felix, Sandi Fox, Gladys Grace, Virginia Gunn, Nancy Halpern, Carla Hassel, Sandra Hatch, Helen Kelley, Jean Ray Laury, Terry Mangat, Mary Mashuta, Suellen Meyer, Barbara Moll, Jan Myers-Newbury, Yvonne Porcella, Joan Schulze, Maria McCormick Snyder, Pan Studstill, and Judith Weissman.

Morning lectures were also presented at the pier, the location of the Festival itself. The distinguished presenters for these included: Mary Mashuta, Nancy Paskin, Barbara Schaffeld, Irma Shore, Phyllis Tepper, Bev Vickery, and Shelly Zegart.

In addition, a range of evening activities was planned for Festival participants. "Quilting Around the World," directed by Susan Faeder, provided a wonderful opportunity to meet international quilters and leave with a unique memento of the evening. It included a slide show of quilts from around the world, a lecture on the state of quiltmaking in various nations, and an International Parade of Quilters with their quilts, and an International Nine-Patch Exchange.

Barbara Moll and Moneca Calvert coordinated "Show and Share," a "show-off" of quilters' best and worst pieces and a sharing of their triumphs and disasters with fellow quilters.

Mary Ellen Hopkins, well known for her trunk shows, put together "Getting a Drink Out of a Fire

Hose," a presentation of quilting anecdotes mixed with invaluable advice on quilting techniques.

Elizabeth Warren put together a series of rich and informative exhibitions of antique and contemporary quilts to complement the centerpiece contest exhibition, and several recent additions to the permanent collection of the museum were included.

The exhibition, "The Romance of Double Wedding Ring Quilts," included twenty-six quilts in the ever-popular Double Wedding Ring pattern. Each quilt was excitingly different from the others. These quilts, plus many others in the Double Wedding Ring design, are illustrated in a new book by Robert Bishop, which also includes several patterns and full instructions that were developed by Carter Houck.

Another special exhibition planned for the Festival and coordianted by Donna Wilder was "Quilts Japan," the first American presentation of the top ten prizewinning quilts from a Japanese contest for contemporary quiltmakers.

During the time of the Festival, nearly 150 exhibitors offered for sale antique and contemporary quilts, craft-related items, quilt supplies, and an incredible array of related textiles—in short, a marketplace of splendid temptations for quilters and quilt lovers.

Organizing The Great American Quilt Festival 2 was an exciting but challenging experience; it would have been impossible to accomplish this task alone and, therefore, many people are to be thanked for their participation:

—The contest itself was made possible by the generous support of three wonderful sponsors: Fairfield Processing Corporation/Poly-fil®, Spring-maid®, and Coats and Clark, Inc./Dual Duty Plus® Quilting Thread.

—The Vista International Hotel, where our final judging for the Memories of Childhood contest took place, also graciously provided the rooms for the winners of the grand prizes during their stay in New York City for the Festival.

—Our panel of judges were complete professionals, and their excitement and enthusiasm about the quilts was catching. Their flexibility and good humor made the judging process a delight. The judges were: Moneca Calvert, Grand Prize Winner, 1986 Great American Liberty Quilt Contest; Jeff Gutcheon, architect/designer, quiltmaker, and New York quilt retailer; Carter Houck, editor of *Lady's Circle Patchwork Quilts*; Lawrence Kane, senior editor for *Family Circle Magazine*; Bonnie Leman, founder and editor-in-chief of *Quilter's Newsletter Magazine*; Cyril I. Nelson, compiler of *The Quilt Engagement Calendar*; Donna Wilder, director of marketing, Fairfield Processing Corporation, organizer of Wearable Art Fashion Show; and Elizabeth V. Warren, curator of the Museum of American Folk Art and author of *Young America: A Folk-Art History*.

—Many hands make light work. A very true statement in this case, for the capable hands of Susan Faeder, Janey Fire, Karla Friedlich, Ann Marie Reilly, and Karen Walsh helped to display the quilts and greatly facilitated the judging process.

—All of the interviews for this book were done by Jacqueline M. Atkins, Jeanne Carley, Susan Faeder, Edith Garshman, Paula Laverty, and Mimi Sherman. Their efforts have provided us with warm and insightful profiles of the winning quilters. Jacquie Atkins also did a masterful job in coordinating, rewriting, and editing the texts for this book.

—Without the wonderful support of Robert Bishop, director, and the staff of the Museum of American Folk Art and the staff of Sanford L. Smith and Associates, Ltd., major-event producers and managers, mounting the contest and the Festival would have been an impossible task. The opportunity I have had to play a major part in creating The Great American Quilt Festival 2 has given me some wonderful new memories for the future.

Cathy Rasmussen
Director
The Great American Quilt Festival 2
Museum of American Folk Art

INTRODUCTION

After the phenomenal success of the first Great American Quilt Festival in April 1986, plans for another event were immediately put into motion. Deciding on a theme for the 1989 Festival was a true challenge, however. It seemed impossible to compete with the appeal and importance of the Statue of Liberty, the hundredth anniversary of which was the celebratory theme of the first quilt contest, and so much time and energy went into finding an appropriate and exciting direction for the second contest. When the idea of using crib quilts was proposed, it seemed the problem was solved!

No one can deny the universal appeal of crib quilts. Even those who have no interest in large-scale quilts admit that the smaller versions have a captivating charm that few can resist. As the Museum of American Folk Art's collection of crib quilts has always met with an enthusiastic response during its travels, the museum staff felt confident that a contest based on this size quilt would appeal to everyone.

The crib-quilt concept also conformed to the museum's intention to have the contest revolve around a traditional form, but one that would allow enough space for freedom of expression through contemporary design. The staff also hoped that the more manageable size, although requiring as much creativity as a large quilt, would provide more encouragement to the novice quilter and the first-time contest entrant, as well as provide a challenge to the more experienced quilter.

Once the idea of using crib quilts was accepted, the theme "Memories of Childhood" seemed to be a natural one. Everyone would certainly be able to identify with this theme, and exploring memories of the past could be fun. As each individual has different recollections of his or her own childhood, a great diversity of design could be expected, leading ultimately to a great exhibition of fascinating contrasts. We were on our way!

Announcements of the contest were made in July 1987. The contest was set to begin officially on September 1, 1987, and last for one year, with the closing deadline scheduled for September 1, 1988. With this amount of time, as many quilters as possible could enter the contest.

The excitement of the staff about "Memories of Childhood" was overshadowed by the tremendous response of the press. Because this contest was to be both a national and an international event, each state and many countries wanted their residents to be aware of it, and the release announcing the contest was picked up by newspapers across the country. The prize money—$7,500 for first place, $5,000 for second place, and $2,500 for third place—made the contest even more appealing news. Every quilting publication that was contacted, both here and abroad, as well as several family, home decorating, and country-style magazines, included something about the contest. The news was even covered in child and parenting publications!

Confident that the word was out successfully, the museum staff then waited, with some anxiety, to see how it would be received. It was a very short wait, and the volume of mail in response was staggering. Thousands and thousands of requests for rules came from quilters around the world. Not only did they ask for the rules, but they wrote about themselves and their families. The letters were warm and personal and gave glimpses into people's everyday lives. Quilters from all over related their enthusiasm for the contest and their excitement about The Great American Quilt Festival 2. It became apparent that we were all linked by a common interest—quilting.

After the months of promotional effort, it was quite a thrill to see the color slides—the first step in the

1

contest judging—of the finished quilts start to arrive in March 1988. As the contest deadline approached, once again the museum's mailbags were filled to overflowing with entries representing every part of the United States and many different countries.

More than 1200 entries were received by the time the deadline came around. The museum staff reviewed the slides as they came in, and a real sense of the time, effort, and feelings that went into each quilt was evident. It was easy to establish a personal connection with many of the designs, as they struck familiar chords within each person's memory.

The great variety of images used to depict the "Memories of Childhood" theme was exciting. Memories of their own childhood were reactivated for many quilters in viewing their children in similar situations. Many people depicted memories of the Depression, others of World War II. Favorite toys, books, people, and places—even TV shows!—were lovingly captured in fabric. Special vacation memories of long ago were relived and framed in a cloth photograph album. Life on the farm and attending class in a one-room schoolhouse were still vivid recollections for many quilters. Special friends, beloved grandparents, and neighbors from long ago were fondly remembered and documented in original ways. Childhood outings, festivals and events, favorite fairy tales and book characters, and loved toys were universal themes for national and international entrants alike.

It was fascinating to see the quilters beautifully capture the memory of an especially meaningful person or event in time. In the frenzied and anxious world of today, the significance of giving permanency to a memory from a less-hurried and reflective period became very important for a majority of the quilters.

Judging from the quilters' descriptions of their memories—and of themselves—the entrants ran the gamut of age and occupation; there were grandmothers (grandfathers, too!), retirees, new mothers, working women, quilt-contest lovers, quilt enthusiasts, quilt-contest winners, and many who were entering a contest for the very first time. They proved to be a true cross section of the population, underlining the universality of the craft.

Contest requirements called for piecing, appliqué, or embroidery to be used on the quilt tops; these could be used alone or in combination with one another, and then the whole piece had, of course, to be quilted. Many of the entrants elected to combine techniques in order to produce a greater effect in the design. Although embroidery was used on a number of quilts for detailing and outlining, appliqué and piecing were naturally the techniques most frequently employed by the quilters.

The imaginative use of photo transfers was a technique present in some quilts and brought an added dimension to them. Stencils and fabric painting were used by many quilters for outlining, highlighting, and illustrating facial features. The use of paint seemed to allow greater artistic expression and quite often combined a sense of the traditional with the contemporary.

Color, of course, was of first importance in the design of most of the quilts. For many of the quilters, the significance of certain colors was crucial, as they were symbolic of special memories from their childhoods. In those cases where a quilter was striving for a particular effect through color and shading, the fabrics were often hand-dyed if the desired color was not readily available.

Perhaps conforming to the concept of traditional quilting, the most widely used fabric for the quilts was cotton. Many entrants also used common as well as innovative embellishments for theme emphasis and design enhancement. Metallic fabrics, velvets, satins, and laces were used in a variety of ways. Beads, netting, ribbons, special borders, and removable stuffed figures allowed imaginations to explore new avenues.

From the variety and range of the entries, it was clear from early in the process that picking winners would be an important and fascinating task, demanding difficult choices to be made. The judges rose to the occasion, shouldering with enthusiasm their responsibility to determine which of the many beautiful quilts would be the winners.

Each quilt was to be evaluated on its originality, the execution of the theme, the overall appearance, the craftsmanship, and its needlework. The initial judging was done at the museum over a period of two days from slides submitted with each entry—one of the quilt as a whole and three showing details. Two semifinalists were selected from each state and foreign countries. In some instances, the decision was so difficult that three semifinalists were chosen.

After the slide judging was completed, all of the semifinalists were contacted by phone and asked to send their quilts to the museum for the final judging. It was a pleasure for the museum staff to be able to relay the happy news and hear the reactions of the semifinalists. As the quilts began to arrive from all over the world, many turned out to be even more exciting than the slides had promised. The final judging clearly was going to be an even greater challenge than we originally had thought!

All of the quilts arrived safely, some just in the nick of time for the judging. After two days of consideration, the panel selected the finalist from each state (in the case of Colorado and Utah, the decision proved so difficult that cofinalists were picked) and participating country, the judges' choices, quilts to receive special achievement awards, and of course, the three grand prize winners. Not an easy task and one that required hard work and much concentration!

The first showing of these wonderful winning quilts was set for The Great American Quilt Festival 2 in New York City on April 26–30, 1989, and the quilts will tour the country for three years after the festival. Each of the quilts in the "Memories of Childhood" exhibition makes a special statement about childhood that has been transformed into a small fabric painting. They allow us glimpses into people's lives as well as an opportunity to look back at our own childhood experiences. For those who may not have the chance to view the splendid quilts in person, the photographs in this book have beautifully captured their charm and special flavor. They are a tangible reminder of those childhood memories that we all hold dear.

ROBERT BISHOP
Director
Museum of American Folk Art

Aunt Helen's Chest of Treasures by Barbara Taylor, Florence, Alabama. 1988. 53″ x 43″. Polyester/cotton. When the artist first heard about this quilt contest, she immediately conceived the idea of paying tribute to her adored Aunt Helen, her mother's sister who had lived with the family during the Depression years and who, she recalls, was "instrumental in my life." Barbara Taylor particularly cherishes her childhood memory of Aunt Helen cleaning out her large and decorative walnut chest once a year and giving the young Barbara choice items from it. It was this scene that she chose to depict with an entranced version of her younger self happily watching as her aunt sorts through her precious trove. "As a little girl, I just couldn't wait to get all the fabulous treasures my aunt gave me when she cleaned out her chest!" Aunt Helen also did superb needlework; the artist used her as a role model and credits her aunt for her proficiency in crewel work, a sample of which can be seen in the wallpaper frieze in the room scene. This quilt, which also uses both appliqué and embroidery, gives clear evidence of her skills; it is the first quilt that the artist has done from scratch. "It was not planned in its entirety— it just grew. Every aspect of the quilt was a challenge that had to be solved on the spot." When the quilter wanted to find a way to present the message of the quilt, for example, she experimented in many ways before arriving at the idea of using a sampler (hanging on the wall) on which she embroidered "Oh, rich are the pleasures of a chest bursting with treasures," an appropriate and effective vehicle for this purpose. Barbara Taylor had to plan her quilting time around her full-time job as a schoolteacher as well as around the frequent visits of her grandchildren. She found that she took the quilt with her wherever she went so that any spare moments could be devoted to it. The artist also writes a column called "The Middle Ages" for a local paper, *The Times Daily*. The title refers to her time of life, and the column is a humorous view of her job and family.

Nessie of Neva Strait by Janine Holzman, Sitka, Alaska. 1988. 54″ x 47″. Cotton. This quilt not only features a friendly, nautical subject, Nessie the sea monster, it was also actually quilted at sea. The artist and her husband fish for a living, and they are frequently away from home for weeks at a time during the fishing season. "The way it works with fishing is that there are a few times during the day when you may have some time for yourself. You know your time is limited, so you need to make the most of it if you want to quilt. You can't go on quilting binges." Janine Holzman taught herself how to quilt, but she credits her grandmother, who was a quilter, with providing the inspiration for this endeavor. She remembers the fun of sitting on the bed and playing games with quilt fabrics when she was a child; those memories led to the idea of making a Charm quilt from many, many bits of fabric. Although each piece of fabric in a Charm quilt is supposed to be different, traditionally the maker cheats a little by putting in a duplicate swatch so children can play at finding it, and this artist followed tradition. However, there are over 421 separate fabrics in the quilt! Fan blocks were used to form the continuous curve of Nessie's body, and the artist feels that this gives the quilt a unique flavor. Janine Holzman found that Nessie's head turned out to be the most difficult part of making the quilt; she was unhappy with the first head she made and then had to spend time at the library looking at children's books until she found a satisfactory illustration on which to base her final rendition. She enjoyed reliving the memories the quilt evoked: monsters may abound in the sea lore of Alaska, but she recalls stories of a relative of Nessie lurking in Flathead Lake, Montana, near where she grew up. The quilter teaches patchwork quilting at Islands Community College and is a member of the Ocean Wave Quilters, both located in Sitka. She has won Best of Show and Viewer's Choice awards at the South East Alaska State Fair and has exhibited in the Alaska State Museum's fiber art show.

Little Bear on the Prairie by Linda Aiken, Phoenix, Arizona. 1988. 53″ x 45″. Cotton. To this very avid teddy-bear collector, cuddly, plump teddy bears "mean the joy of childhood." Linda Aiken grew up in Kansas, and she has chosen to depict this happy teddy bear, whose heart is stuffed with love, surrounded by Kansas mementoes. A maple tree, sunflowers, wheat fields, delicate grape hyacinths, and fluttering butterflies all reflect the natural surroundings that she enjoyed so much as a child. The artist recalls that "there was a maple tree in our front yard, and when the grape hyacinths appeared beneath the tree, it was a sure sign of spring." Her father cared for their beautiful yard, and it provided the setting for some very happy moments in the artist's childhood. Linda Aiken and her mother learned to quilt together from an article that they had read in *Woman's Day* magazine about ten years ago. Since then, the artist has done ten wall quilts. She uses a stab-stitch technique in her quilting that she admits is time-consuming but that she prefers nevertheless. The highly textured fabric used for the teddy bear and the thin strips of contrasting fabrics done with reverse-appliqué on the bark of the tree give both a sense of depth and texture to the quilt. There were times when the artist became discouraged while she was working on *Little Bear on the Prairie* because it seemed to be taking so long to complete. However, her friends were all so very supportive and encouraging that she pushed herself to complete the project. The quilter, who is employed full-time as the manager of a greeting-card and gift shop, worked evenings and weekends on the quilt, but found that she needed more time. In order to meet the deadline she had to take a week off from work, but the final product was well worth the effort. The self-taught artist exhibits and sells her work through the Quilted Apple, a local quilt shop; several years ago she won a third place award for one of her quilts at the Arizona State Fair.

My Childhood Memories: Mary Janes and Peter Pans by Lucinda S. Livingston, Van Buren, Arkansas. 1988. 52″ x 43½″. Cotton, buttons. The artist presents a nostalgic remembrance of little-girl dressing in this creative interpretation of plain white Peter Pan collars topping a variety of print dresses worn with Mary Jane shoes. These simple elements combine to form an unusually attractive overall image. "Mine was an orderly childhood, a happy parade of shiny black shoes and pockets full of posies," the artist notes. She recalls that she really would have preferred at least one pair of red patent-leather shoes when she was a little girl, but her mother always bought her black Mary Janes. "I was tempted to mingle a pair of red shoes with all the black Mary Janes waltzing around the quilt border," she says, but she finally decided against it because she felt the meaning would be too esoteric. Working on the quilt and thinking back over her childhood caused the artist to realize just how much her mother had influenced her thinking and helped to determine her values; many years later she found herself dressing her own daughter in the same conservative way that her mother had dressed her. Lucinda Livingston has been quilting since 1985, and this was the first quilt contest that she had ever entered. She was intrigued by the criterion of originality and felt it posed a real challenge to her. She believes that "a quilt does not necessarily have to be a preplanned work of art," but that its spirit ought to be spontaneous and also guided by the materials available to the quilter. She is partial to overall patterns, and this is reflected in her work. The artist plans to save the quilt for a grandchild, as she is practical and wants it to be used as well as viewed. She is a member of the Belle Point Quilters Guild in Fort Smith, Kansas, the American Quilters Society, and the National Quilting Association. She squeezes quilting time in between her work as a biomedical electronics technician and study for a degree in Women's Studies.

A Mother's Dream by Linda K. O'Dell, Bakersfield, California. 1987–1988. 54″ x 45″. Cotton, some lamés. *Judge's Choice.* This is the first quilt that Linda K. O'Dell, a professional fiber artist, has made. Working on the quilt helped the artist to cope with the death of her father and gave her "the opportunity to learn so much about myself. The quilt represents a great deal of remembering of just how wonderful my childhood was and how wonderful it also is for my children today. It represents an ideal of what all parents strive for: giving your children special memories to be cherished that they, given the opportunity, will in turn give to their children."

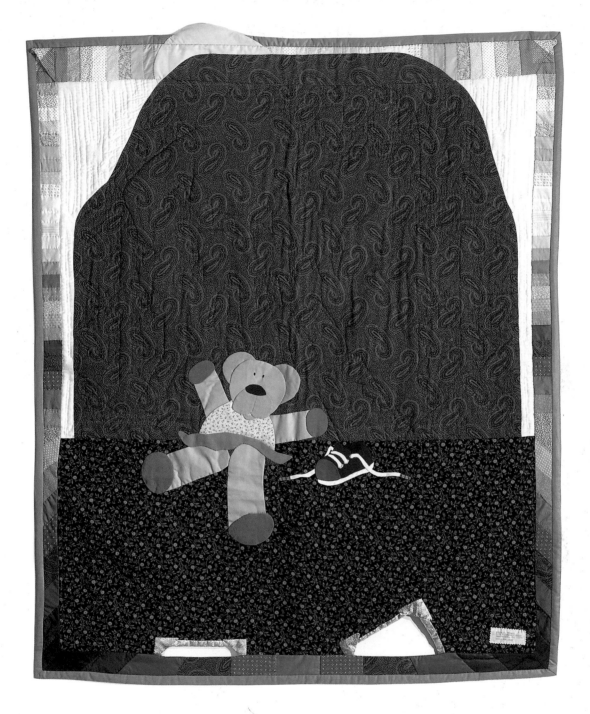

Her father's loss had evoked a number of memories and led her to a deepening awareness of the difficulties of being a parent. In this quilt, the exhausted mother drowsing in a chair with her children cuddled close is a symbol of the fact that parenting is hard work! The photographs tumbling from the album on the mother's lap were created from a blend of childhood memories of her husband, herself, and their children. One is actually based on a photo of the artist's older daughter proudly holding a chicken; the others show scenes that are all part of growing up: potty training, a birthday party, a ball game, learning to read. The quilted photos are framed in lamé representing gold and silver "because memories are precious and deserve to be framed in precious metals." At the bottom of the quilt two empty frames represent the unknown future. The back of the quilt gives yet another facet of the scene: the mother's head shows just over the back of the chair, and a teddy bear and a pair of sneakers have slipped behind and rest unnoticed. This untidiness underlines the fact that "mothers are not perfect, but they try their best." In her regular column "The Needle and I" for the *Bakersfield Californian*, the artist provided readers with a step-by-step description of how *A Mother's Dream* was designed and executed, down to the "jelly stains provided by her youngest daughter while patiently watching Mommy 'quilck.'"

Our Trip to Florida by Patty Hawkins, Lyons, Colorado. 1988. 55″ x 46″. Satin, cotton, cotton/polyester blends. *Judge's Choice.* For a little girl living in Shreveport, Louisiana, going all the way to Florida for a vacation and a chance to see the ocean was "an unbelievably exciting event." There was no question in Patty Hawkins's mind, once she decided to enter the contest, that this would be the childhood memory she would depict in her quilt. But she did not want to rely solely on her own memories of the experience; she contacted relatives who had accompanied her on that early Florida trip and asked them what their recollections were. Sharing these experiences gave the family a new perspective about what the journey had meant to each of them. One incident in particular stood out in the artist's memory: she vividly remembers seeing a Seminole Indian woman coming out of a department store and being "mesmerized" by the brilliance and intricacy of the woman's voluminous skirt. Patty Hawkins firmly believes that she was "meant to see that woman" so that someday she could use her in a quilt. The skirt that so astonished the artist as a twelve-year-old child has been re-created in the quilt using the Seminole patchwork technique and layers of hand-sewn ricrac. A "postcard" giving the key to the location; scenes of the Seven-Mile Bridge, flamingoes, the artist and her sister at the beach; and "captions" reinforce the photo-album impression of this quilt. Patty Hawkins loves to quilt in a contemporary style; she strives to be creative, and, for her, this means "getting out of the cocoon of tradition." She has been greatly encouraged in her endeavors by her quilting group as well as by her husband—during her quilting "binges" (as she terms them) to get the quilt ready for the contest, her husband "even ironed his own shirts" to help out! The artist is a member of the American International Quilt Association, the Colorado Quilt Council, the East Bay Heritage Quilters, the American Quilters Society, and the Art Quiltists Design Group.

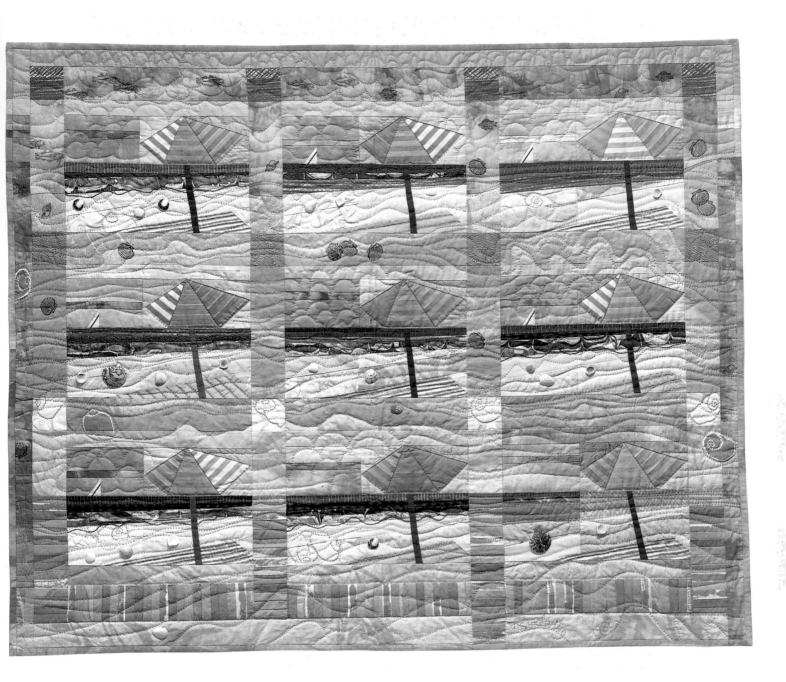

I'm Going Up the Beach by Marguerite Malwitz, Brookfield, Connecticut. 1988. 45″ x 54½″. Cotton, cotton/polyester, silk, metallic threads, rubber stamps, shells. The artist believes that it is quite a miracle that this quilt came to be. She did not originally plan to enter the quilt contest; she had designed ten small blocks with the intention of framing and selling them individually. In June, however, almost at the last minute, she decided to enter and, with the encouragement of her husband, began to work frantically to meet the contest deadline. Marguerite Malwitz began quilting two years ago after experiencing a mid-life crisis and physical depression. Then, as now, she believes that God gave her help by inspiring her to try quilting and to use His Creation as a theme. Therefore, the quilter often depicts natural features such as the beach or the desert in her works. In this crib quilt, the maker draws on her memories of the New Jersey shore. "Walking up to the beach—or 'up the beach' as they used to say—over the boardwalk (and always awestruck at the vast and changing view), then on to shell collecting at the shoreline" was a very special experience of her childhood. The latter memory is commemorated by the use of real shells in the quilt. The artist attached buttons to the shells by a hot-melting process, then sewed the button/shells to the quilt. Marguerite Malwitz says that she had to use every bit of quilting expertise that she possessed to make this quilt. She has taken quilting workshops with many of the top people in the field and prefers to design and work on her quilts in a contemporary style. She has a background in weaving and has done Jewish ceremonial hangings, one of which hangs in Temple Emanu-El in New York City. The artist is a member of the American Quilters Society, the Nutmeg Guild in Connecticut, and a local group called the Scrap Bag Group. The artist has previously won blue ribbons at a number of shows in New England and New York.

Dream Catcher by Deborah D. Barr, Wilmington, Delaware. 1988. 54″ x 45″. Cotton. Each of the appliquéd images on this quilt represents an event, a person, or a special memory from the artist's childhood, and happy memories mingle with unhappy ones, for childhood is made up of both. The big heart is a dual symbol: it represents both family love and a sister who was born on Valentine's Day. The hypodermic needle, pills, and blood vial are reminders of an extended childhood illness that required continuous blood tests and medication; the deck of cards memorializes a much-loved grandmother who was always fond of a hand of cards; musical images recall important pastimes; the tooth looms large in memory and needs no explanation. The two large hands at the bottom of the quilt—one male, one female—recall Deborah Barr's parents, and the many little hands that reach out from the surrounding border were traced from the hands of the quilter's own children so that they too would become part of the quilt. She wanted her children to relate to the quilt and was very pleased when they showed interest by asking questions about the symbols and images depicted in it. The artist believes that "quilting is a reflective process," and making this quilt brought back an awareness of how much happiness there had been in her early years. The title of the quilt was taken from a song about a spider's web that she remembered learning when she was a child; it contained a description of a web "made to catch a dream and hold it tight until I waken," just as the spiderweb quilting in this quilt cleverly captures its many memories. Deborah Barr has been quilting for ten years and has previously done two full-size quilts and numerous wall hangings. She has exhibited in local quilt shows, and her work has won ribbons over the years. She is a member of the Ladybug Chapter of the National Quilting Association and of the Embroiderers Guild of America. She also writes a regular column on needlework design, called the "Design Sampler," for *Flying Needle* magazine.

Jumping Jacks by Petra Scheibe-Teplitz, Washington, D.C. 1988. 52″ x 44″. Cotton, silk. The bold patterns and strong diagonals that compose these exuberant jumping jacks make them seem ready to jump right out of this quilt toward the viewer. They remind the artist of the ones she enjoyed playing with when she was a child in Hanover, Germany; her childhood jacks had been made out of wood by her father, and she remembers them hanging over her bed, where she could easily reach them for use. These toys in particular are an integral part of the artist's happy memories of childhood. Petra Scheibe-Teplitz, a professional quilter, only recently moved to the District of Columbia from Germany, and she confided that she did take some time off from making this crib quilt in order to do some sightseeing! The artist has been quilting for a number of years and has created over fifty quilts; for the most part, these have been commissioned pieces. The buyer may suggest ideas and colors for a quilt, but the artist prefers to create the design herself. She enjoys working with designs that have a modern and somewhat abstract flavor, and her colors are chosen to add depth and movement to her design, as this quilt aptly demonstrates. Although all piecing and stitching in her quilts is done by hand, the artist does not do what she considers "traditional" quilting in pattern or execution. Silk is one of her favorite fabrics, and she likes to use it in her work because "it shines" and is available in many vibrant colors; she feels that it gives extra texture, luster, and character to her work. She notes that there are few quilt contests in Germany, so it was especially exciting to have the opportunity to enter this one. The artist has shown her work in various galleries in Germany, and some of her current work is being sent back to a shop there for sale. Petra Scheibe-Teplitz came to quilting with an arts background, having studied art at the Kuntschule in Offenbach, Germany, when she was younger.

My Tea Party by Rita Denenberg, Royal Palm Beach, Florida. 1988. 54″ x 45″. Cotton. At first glance, this scene of a little girl sprawled on the floor, reading a favorite book with a cat as her companion, appears typically warm and appealing; yet, on closer scrutiny one becomes aware that the room is barren and empty. There are no furnishings to soften its sparseness, no sign of interaction, no characters in the child's life other than those depicted in the imaginary tea party scene. The quilter has ably used these elements to convey strongly the child's sense of isolation. The artist notes that "reading became an escape from a lonely childhood. While reading *Alice's Adventures in Wonderland*, the tea party became reality outside my room. My books and my cat, Kitchie (shown here in the lower corner of the quilt, wearing the smile of the Cheshire cat), were my only true friends." The little hearts embroidered on the girl's dress remind her of one of the dresses she owned when she was a child. Rita Denenberg believes that making the quilt helped her come to terms with unhappy childhood memories. As a self-taught quilter now teaching others, the artist advises her students to "put yourself into your quilt. Quilting helps you turn negatives into positives." The artist spent three months making the quilt, sometimes working eight to ten hours a day, or "until my eyes gave out." She made two versions of the tea party scene. The first was done without shadows, but she felt that something was missing and remade the whole scene, and then she knew that it was worth the work and effort. Rita Denenberg takes special pleasure in her quilt being chosen to represent the state of Florida, which she dearly loves. She began quilting five years ago and is now a professional quilter. She belongs to the American Quilters Society, the National Quilters Association, and the Palm Beach County Quilters Guild. She is a three-time first prize winner at the South Florida Fair and has won quilt-block contests sponsored by the *Palm Beach Post* and *Quilt Magazine*.

14

Queen Alice by Wendy Analla, Ellabell, Georgia. 1988. 52″ x 43½″. Cotton, cotton blends. *Judge's Choice.* In working "feverishly" to meet the contest deadline, the artist began to carry the quilt with her everywhere, so that not a moment of possible work time would be lost. Soon she found that she had developed a following of both adults and children who eagerly awaited each new development in the quilt. "Sometimes I felt I was dating myself when I chose *Alice's Adventures in Wonderland* for my theme," she noted; several of the young girls in her following were intrigued by the characters, but, to the artist's astonishment, had never heard of Alice and her adventures. This, of course, was soon remedied and Wendy Analla found herself a storyteller as well as a quiltmaker. She remembers that she not only had been fond of the Alice stories when she was a child, she also had been especially smitten with the original illustrations by John Tenniel. In working on this project, she became caught up in the artistic process of attempting to convey a sense of these illustrations in a pictorial quilt. The design actually contains elements from both *Alice's Adventures in Wonderland* and *Through the Looking-Glass.* The artist found that the most difficult part of the quilt was achieving the desired perspective. She used patchwork squares in a checkerboard pattern, but each square had to be individually cut and pieced; she also hand-dyed fabrics to get the gradations in color that help to give the appearance of depth and draw the viewer's eye into the quilt. A stencil brush was used to apply subtle variations of paint for shading; this can be seen on Alice's arms as well as on the unicorn. Wendy Analla is a professional artist and a member of the Arkansas Quilters Guild and the Embroiderers Guild of America. For her, "quilting is an addiction," and she has been rewarded for her addiction with awards from various quilt shows that she has entered, including the Houston International Quilt Festival, the San Antonio Quilt Guild Show, and the Arkansas Quilters Guild Show.

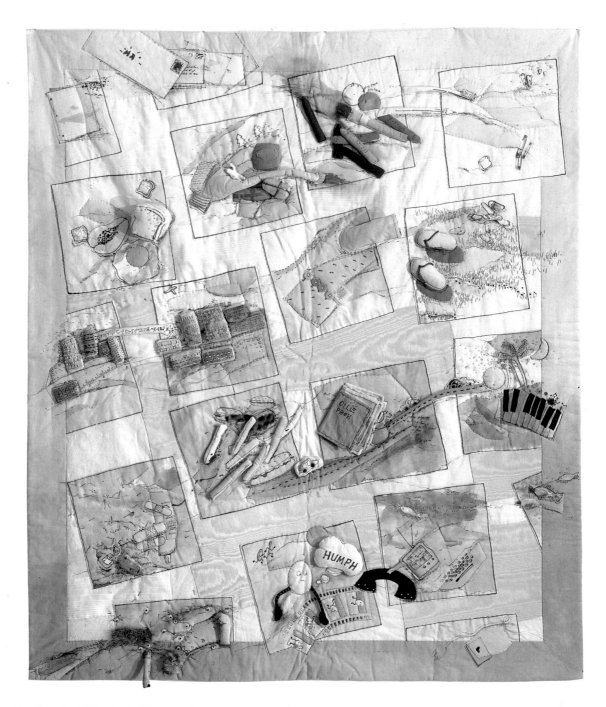

Lea Lovely/Ollie Awful by Wendy Kim Messier, Honolulu, Hawaii. 1988. 53″ x 45″. Cotton, cotton mixture, beads, buttons, muslin backing. In this quilt, Wendy Messier used both specific and abstract imagery to evoke the photographic yet dreamlike quality of images of her daughter's childhood. The artist spent time discussing the imagery with her daughter, who is now seventeen, so that it would contain a truly personal statement for both mother and child. Sickness and fear of the dark are represented by darker areas; the letters are representative of a period when mother and daughter were separated for a long time and their main communication was by mail; the foods (especially the hotdog, hamburger, and french fries) represent favorite things to eat. The slippers, palm trees, and sunshine are typically Hawaiian, while the skyscrapers are reminiscent of trips to New York and Tokyo. The soft and smoky slate greys—a fortuitious blend of fabric, ink, and pencil—that give depth to the quilt reflect a city environment, because the quilter thinks of her daughter as primarily a city person. The best part of quilting for this artist is being able to "illustrate and get an effect with an image." She made a transition from creating soft sculpture to quilting but made use of her sculptural skills in the construction of parts of this quilt. She made extensive use of polyfill stuffing in certain areas of the quilt in order to achieve a more dramatic three-dimensional effect. The title of the quilt is intended to describe the two personalities of Lea, the artist's daughter, when she was a child. She was called Ollie Awful when she was mischievous because her actions and the look on her face reminded her mother of Oliver Hardy; Lea Lovely represented good behavior! The artist says that her daughter is now Lea Lovely all the time and was very pleased to be the subject of the quilt. Wendy Messier exhibited her work at Quilt International 1983 and 1985. She is a member of the Arts Council of Hawaii and earned an MFA in Visual Design from the University of Hawaii.

We Had Paper Dolls...and Our Imaginations by Joyce Winterton Stewart, Rexburg, Idaho. 1988. 54½″ x 45″. Cotton, gold lamé. Three strips of paper dolls recall a special bond between the artist and her brother Wayne. The pair, who are only a year apart in age, came down with measles while the family was living in a motel waiting for a new house they were building to be completed. "Those were the days before TV and video games, and there wasn't a lot to do in such a confined area, even though my parents rented us an extra bedroom. We played games and colored, but the thing I remember best of all was the time Mother went to the store and bought us each some paper dolls. Ordinarily, Wayne wouldn't have really enjoyed playing paper dolls with me and, whenever possible, I would have been more likely to be doing something tomboyish with him. But this was different—we didn't have much else to do—and so we played with our paper dolls for hours each day. We really had to make good use of our imaginations to do this. The time we had to stay inside really did go by much faster because we had paper dolls, each other to play with, and our imaginations!" The paper dolls here are made from single strips of fabric, with no seams joining one to the other; the artist had not done much appliqué before making this quilt, and the paper dolls proved to be much more intricate and difficult than she had expected. She was not happy with the look of the first set and was only satisfied with their appearance after cutting a second set. The folk-art angels flying overhead represent imagination, and the hearts symbolize the love the artist and her brother shared. "We were inseparable throughout our childhood," she recalls. Most of the fabrics are hand-dyed by the artist, and the bias tape in the chain border was handmade as well. Her enthusiasm for her art is infectious, and Joyce Stewart has inspired other family members to begin quilting. She has won many awards for her work and was also Idaho state winner in the Great American Liberty Quilt Contest in 1986.

The World According to Sidney: A Child's Crayon Etching by Sidney Allee Miller, Galena, Illinois. 1988. 45½″ x 54½″. *Creative Interpretation Award.* Cotton, cotton polyester. Through reverse-appliqué, piecework, and embroidery, the artist has captured the pure spirit of a child's drawing in this wonderfully imaginative quilt with its striking colors that seem even more vibrant against the ink-black ground. The design represents a child's perspective of all the ingredients of her immediate neighborhood, including sidewalks, church, houses, people, traffic, pets, flowers, a variety of trees, and even an airplane flying overhead, presented through the suggested medium of a classic child's-art form—a crayon etching. The black ground fabric represents the dark ink overlay that is scratched away in a design to reveal the brilliant crayon colors beneath. After thinking about her design for "months and months," Sidney Miller went to the library and worked out a composite of a child's world from the pictures she found. "I wanted to do something that I liked, that would sustain my interest, and that I thought would be really competitive. I love the way children draw, it's so pure . . . and you forget the way it's done, how they draw trees and houses." Once she had finally worked out the design, the entire quilt was completed in a remarkably short time—only six weeks! "When I had the whole thing put together I was so excited about whether or not it would work that I worked on it until my hands cramped, probably twelve hours or more at once, in order to get one corner done so that I could see what it would look like. It was as much fun for me as it is for a kid who scratches through the ink to find the crayon colors." In addition to her full-time job as a writer and designer for a direct-mail company, Sidney Miller designs wearable art that she sells in her own shop. This is the artist's fifth quilt, and she was also state winner in the Great American Liberty Contest in 1986.

Red Sunglasses 1958 by Lana Trott, Kokomo, Indiana. 1988. 43″ x 52″. Cotton polyester. *Judge's Choice.* This simple yet striking design shows the artist (the girl with pigtails) and her little sister on a bright summer day when they were growing up. The stars on their matching red sunglasses symbolize the hopeful outlook that children share, and the deep blue sky (a recurring theme for the artist) represents the personal and physical space that growing up on a farm provided. The uncluttered design and even the choice of fabric—easy care and washable—are also meant as symbols of the simpler time that childhood represents. The artist had strong memories of old family photographs of the two sisters together, wearing their red terrycloth sunsuits, but after her initial sketch for the quilt was finished, she asked her mother if she could see those photos. Then she found out that things were not quite as she remembered: she could find no photos of the sisters together, they both had ponytails, and shadows obscured their faces! She decided that some poetic license was allowable, however, and so the initial design remained. This is the first original design that Lana Trott has created for a quilt: "I had a feeling of ecstasy about this quilt; while I was doing it I felt as though I were standing on the edge of a high-dive board, getting ready to dive in. It was a very exhilarating and exciting feeling. I had so much fun and enjoyed making this quilt so much. It was a thrill a minute." When she reached the actual quilting, however, the artist panicked. "What am I going to do now?" she would ask herself. "Well, I'll just try this!" The quilting emerged as she went along, and the challenge was ably met. The artist's grandmother, who lived into her nineties, sparked the artist's interest in quilting, and although this is only her fifth completed quilt, she has plans for many more. She is a member of the Indianapolis Art League, and this is the first contest she has entered.

Heritage Quilt: Pieces and the Past by Carla Johnson Hassel, Des Moines, Iowa. 1988. 54½" x 45". Antique and new fabrics; cotton, satin, synthetics. Memories within memories are encompassed in this charming central design of two women savoring a Double Wedding Ring quilt as they share family remembrances while a spider spins lazily in the background. A series of unique heritage blocks, each having a special meaning for the artist, border the quilt and are separated by the repetition of a block called by the artist the "Economy Nine-Patch Variation." The keystone block at the top is stitched but left blank to represent the "unknown" memories of the children of the next generation. Carla Hassel notes that the idea for this quilt had been simmering for years; originally, she had planned to include only one figure, but when she heard about the contest and sat down to do the design, a photograph of her and her daughter relaxing on their front porch made her change her mind. She worked on the quilt almost around the clock over two sultry summer months; "It was a very rough summer," she says. "Drought, deaths in the family, constant visitors, a family reunion—there were periods of sitting and crying and sewing, and the quilt went everywhere with me." She also recalls that "I thought when the lap quilt was done, the rest would be a piece of cake! I thought the heritage blocks would take about a week—instead, they took a month. I somehow forgot, when I decided to do this quilt, that sampler quilts are the hardest of all to do well!" The maker calls this "literally a scrapbag quilt," for there are forty different fabrics in it, and she even took apart an antique quilt top—something she normally will not do, no matter how worn the piece—to get the right fabrics for two of the heritage blocks. The artist has lost track of the number of quilts she has made, but many have appeared at state fairs and in juried shows. She has authored two books on quilting and one on the appliqué art of the Hmong of southeast Asia, and she is a member of the Iowa Quilters Guild.

I Remember Daydreaming by Lori Backes, Wichita, Kansas. 1988. 54″ x 45″. Cotton, cotton polyester. "All children at one time or another pretend that their toys are alive," says the artist, "and what better place for them to come alive than in a toy shop!" Lori Backes got her inspiration for this sprightly scene from a Christmas card she received several years ago. The toys clamber from the shelves of the shop, ready for fun and games while no one watches them. A teddy bear prances across the floor, a doll waves her arms in glee, the hobby horse gallops, the panda agilely climbs from shelf to floor, and a toy plane appears ready for take-off. The moon and the stars on this magical night seem to float right through the window of the shop. On the right side of the quilt a large, stuffed-work crayon seems to color in the entire scene, as though this were a page in a coloring book, and stitching is used to create an energetic collage of circles, squares, and triangles that tumble around the border fabric that serves as a frame for the scene. This quilt represents the artist's first attempt at appliqué, and she readily admits that "it was very frustrating." The piecework required for the shelves, toys, and windows was complicated and very difficult, but a good learning experience. As a full-time new-accounts representative for a bank and mother to a lively three-year-old, Lori Backes finds that her quilting time tends to come late at night; she has also been known to spend her lunch hours and breaks at work quilting if a project needed the time. She was given her first sewing machine when she was ten years old and has been sewing ever since; she has, however, only been quilting for five years and has made eight quilts in that time. This quilt, her first contest entry, survived two house moves and her husband's architectural exams during its construction! The artist, a member of the Prairie Quilt Guild, is now looking forward to the challenge of designing quilts on a computer.

It Was All So Black and White by Teresa Tucker Young, Georgetown, Kentucky. 1988. 55″ x 44″. Cotton. *Creative Interpretation Award.* Teresa Young approached the problem of picking a theme for her quilt as a search for a particular childhood memory for "someone of my generation that would be different from the memories of someone of any other time and group." Once she realized that her generation was the first to grow up with the significant presence of television in the home and that, for a long period, only black-and-white TV programs were available to them, the theme for her quilt became obvious. The two pajama-clad children sitting engrossed in the adventures of Superman on the large and bulky 1950s-style TV set at the center of the quilt represent the artist and her brother; the smaller sets floating around them show images of many other favorite children's TV characters and programs of the period: Captain Kangaroo, the Lone Ranger, Howdy Doody, Mickey Mouse, and Lucy. Nor are the ubiquitous commercials forgotten: Tony the Tiger; Snap, Crackle, and Pop; and a jug of Kool-Aid all immediately bring to mind the products and their associated characters that were also part of growing up in the pioneer days of TV viewing. Each TV set represents a popular brand of the time, and the three major networks—almost all that was available before the explosion of cable TV—are included as well. For accuracy, the artist researched advertisements and television shows of the 1950s and 1960s at the University of Kentucky library; the use of only black, white, and grey fabrics throughout the quilt subtly and effectively underlines her message. Teresa Young has been quilting seriously since 1985; her work has been exhibited in several art galleries, at the National Quilt Association Show, and at the American Quilters Society Show in Paducah, Kentucky. She came to quilting from a background in art, and her special talent is nostalgic pictorial narrative work, a good example of which is evident in this winning quilt.

The Gift of Flowers by Susie Weber Drell, Alexandria, Louisiana. 1988. 56″ x 45″. Muslin, cotton, voile. Susie Drell has created a beautiful whole-cloth quilt appliquéd with a delicate wreath of pastel flowers and bows. It symbolizes an important event in her childhood when the family lived on a military base in Alabama: "When I was ten, my father had surgery in a military hospital near our home. Daily, I pulled a wagon full of flowers into his ward and gave them to my father and other patients. These flowers are now seen through the haze of time." Shadow appliqué—laying voile over the appliquéd design and then quilting it to the muslin ground of the piece—is the technique used to give the soft and misty quality reminiscent of other times to the quilt. The artist has always had a special love of flowers and remembers that her three teenagers also seemed always to be carrying flowers around when they were children. "Fortunately," she notes, "we live in a place where flowers bloom all year round." In designing the quilt, Susie Drell remembered that "as a child, I never had a quilt. I thought, if I were a baby, what I would want one to look like. It came out just the way I wanted!" She is thrilled to think that one day a baby may, in fact, sleep under her quilt. The artist also wanted to create a quilt that would emphasize her fine quilt stitching (she credits her grandmother with passing along the talent to quilt eleven to twelve stitches to the inch), and this quilt is indeed a tour de force in that area. When the artist began quilting only two years ago, she already was a skilled needlewoman in hand sewing, needlepoint, and cross-stitch, and her abilities in this new area have already won her numerous awards—in fact, each quilt she has made has been a winner. She is a member of the Patience Quilting Guild, the Gulf State Quilters Association, and the National Quilters Association, and she volunteers her time to demonstrate quilting at a nearby restored farmhouse museum. As she says, "When your fingers are busy, your mind can just soar."

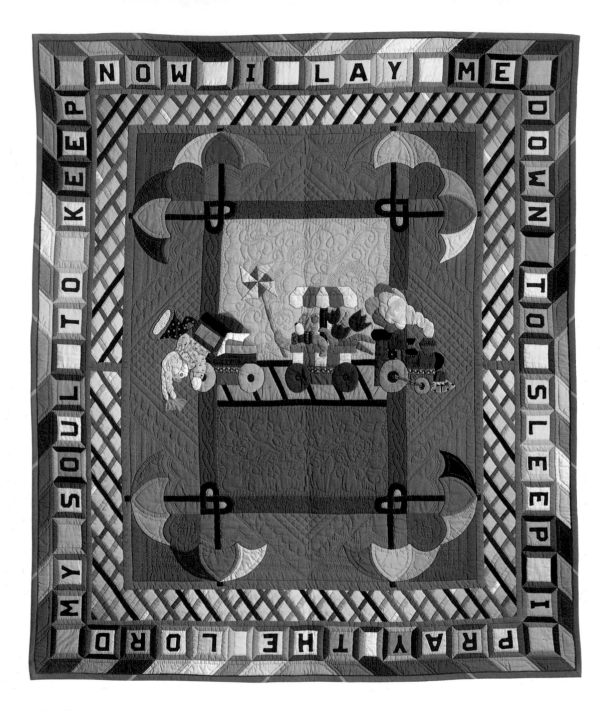

...As I Fall Asleep by Dianne Hire, Belfast, Maine. 1988. 54″ x 45″. Cotton, cotton polyester. According to the artist, the title refers to "a child's recounting of the day's flurry of activities—from seeing rainy-day umbrellas out of a lattice-covered window to ragdolls and trains laden with tulips and toys to the child's prayer before drifting into slumber." The umbrellas with their intertwined handles forming hearts were the artist's starting images as she planned the design during a car trip from Maine to the Amish country around Lancaster, Pennsylvania. Other images came in various ways: "I spent time in the library, sitting in the children's section flipping through children's books, as well as perusing all the books of my friends' kids to see what the toys should look like and to trigger better ideas. Also, I asked my friends for their favorite childhood memories, so this was a compilation of ideas from many sources." As the quilt evolved during its construction, Dianne Hire felt a strong conviction that her religious beliefs should be part of it: "Every single step has been a prayer to help me through this quilt. It was a complete reliance on faith. I would run out of fabric and have to travel all over the state to find a replacement. I would have to change midstream to something new. It was a complete agony all the way through, but it was always better than I had conceived." Originally the baby blocks around the border had contained the alphabet, but at three o'clock one morning the artist had the idea to replace that with the Child's Prayer, and with some squeezing and a few small adjustments, it fit! Dianne Hire is a founding member of her local quilt guild, Friendship Samplers, and a member of the Pine Tree Quilt Guild and the American Quilters Society. Her love and talent for quilting is inherited from her grandmother, who began teaching her how to piece in 1985; her use of solid, crisp colors is a result of her love of Amish design; and the central rectangle of this quilt shows further Amish influence—perhaps a result of that trip to Pennsylvania!

Alphabet Sampler Quilt by Carol H. Gersen, Boonsboro, Maryland. 1988. 53″ x 46½″. Cotton. At a show several years ago, a German quilter remarked to Carol Gersen how lucky Americans were to have a tradition to draw on for their quilting; the artist realized that this was something she had always taken for granted and so, in considering the design for this contest, she decided to reach into the past. "I have taken something from the past and made it my modern interpretation of a really old-fashioned pattern. I've simplified it, enlarged it; I've used a combination of my own hand-dyed fabrics as well as bolt goods. I have a lot more control over my medium than they did long ago." The artist realized that eighteenth- and nineteenth-century samplers fit better into her graphic piecing method than the early appliqué alphabet quilting patterns she had first intended to use, and so she decided to concentrate on them. They also appealed to her because "I love words, books, reading. Learning the alphabet and how to read as a child opened a great world to me." She researched samplers at the library, designed all of her letters on graph paper, then did a master drawing. The background was cut out first, then each piece of each letter—nearly two thousand pieces in all! One difficulty that arose was the stifling heat that characterized the summer of 1988. The artist could not open a window or use a fan for fear of all those little pieces—now organized on a white felt wall—flying elsewhere. Carol Gersen has used an original approach by introducing a Nine Patch pattern into the center of each letter as a constant horizontal element. The free-form, curvilinear hand-quilting pattern offers contrast and softens the rigid squares and rectangles comprising the quilt. The artist became a serious quilter in 1977 when she lived in rural Maine and studied at the Haystack School. She exhibits widely in juried shows and belongs to many quilter's groups, including the Fiber Arts Study Group in Washington, D.C., and the New Images Quilters Group.

Blackout on Beacon Street by Kathleen Weinheimer, Bridgewater, Massachusetts. 1988. 54″ x 45″. Cotton. *Judge's Choice.* "I have a vague memory of an eerie light and I was terrified of the chimney pots. I was about three years old at the time," relates the artist in discussing this dramatic quilt. And the chimney pots do indeed loom ominously against a hint of brightness from the rising moon in this quilt that recalls the blackouts in Boston during World War II and represents the view from the artist's bedroom window. Kathleen Weinheimer has succinctly captured the brooding sense of those long and—to a three-year-old—frightening nights in her sparse, impressionistic design that relies on a careful choice of shaded fabrics to convey the overall mood. The delicate, flowery prints that are used extensively throughout the quilt provide a sharp and intriguing contrast to the somber sense they create as a whole. Her clever selection of background prints further hints at the extensiveness and complexity of the city, and the curvilinear quilting gives an underlying sense of motion and excitement. The red pinwheel symbolizes the artist's presence—a small glow of energy and life in the surrounding darkness. "This was not meant to be a pretty quilt. It was a gut-feeling piece, one that just came right out. It was one of the easiest quilts I've ever put together." It took her only six weeks to complete, and she notes that "I had to keep checking with my dad on what was real versus what was imagined and what the windows looked like." The artist teaches quilting in the public school system at night and in her home during the daytime. She credits one of her students with encouraging her to enter this contest. Her work has been extensively shown in the fifteen years that she has been quilting; in addition to shows in New England and the Schweinfurth Art Center in Auburn, New York, the artist has had a quilt shown every year at the American Quilters Society Show in Paducah, Kentucky.

Instamatic Ponies by Isolde Sarnecki-de Vries, Ann Arbor, Michigan. 1988. 53½″ x 43½″. Cotton, gold lamé, silk. Dream and reality intermingle in this highly imaginative and skillful quilt picture of a young girl astride a galloping carousel horse that seems to want to run right off the quilt, while many other appliquéd and quilted horses, each appearing to have a life of its own, cavort in the starry night skies behind them. The artist, the mother of three children below the age of six, found her inspiration for this quilt's theme in her children's love of carousels and in the many family photos of them enjoying the merry-go-round. Isolde Sarnecki-de Vries also has fond memories of her own childhood days in the Netherlands, where family outings to the fair and its carousel were always a special treat. The bright colors the artist has used in the main figures provide a sharp contrast to the greys, whites, and blacks of the "photo negatives" of yet more carousel horses, some of whom continue their ride off the film strips and into the intricate background quilting. The colorful border contains a series of red-and-white carnival tents. The quilt accurately captures a child's sense of wonder and joy at the magical carousel as it emits a glowing sense of mystery, excitement, and, perhaps, just a hint of fear. The quilt seems barely able to contain all the action, and some of the images extend beyond its rectangular parameters. Except for the tiny squares running along the edges of the "negatives," each row of which took her at least a day to complete, this quilt "came" easily to the artist and she loved making it. The artist is a member of the Greater Ann Arbor Quilt Guild and was the Michigan state winner in the Great American Liberty Quilt Contest in 1986. Although she had long been drawn to big graphic designs on quilts, she had never really thought of quilting as an art form until she saw two television shows on quilting in 1984. She then became really excited by the great possibilities that she felt quilting offered. "I haven't even really gotten started yet," she says.

Time's Treasury by Maria A. Forcier, Minneapolis, Minnesota. 1988. 54″ x 45½″. Cotton. The artist's most vivid memories of her childhood are of the happy days she spent on her aunt's farm. That farm, with its whitewashed frame house, its big red barn and towering silo, set amid gently rolling hills and fields with a majestic mountain looming in the distance, forms the core of the memories expressed in this quilt. Inset vignettes of other childhood joys—a bluebird singing in the morning, an open window where freshly baked pies were set to cool, a child entranced with the fragrance and beauty of a flower, long walks through the fields—all add to the special charm and appeal of this quilt. The combination of greens, golds, and browns in the foreground and middle distance immediately generate a sense of the warmth and security of the rural setting, while the dark tones used for the mountain add the contrast of distance and mystery. To create a feeling of depth and distance, the artist appliquéd the quilt from the top down and used strong and flowing lines of stitching in the plowed fields to reinforce the effect even further. Maria Forcier, at age twenty-six one of the contest's youngest entrants, began to quilt seriously after taking a course on the many uses of textiles while she was working on her bachelor's degree at the University of Wisconsin at Stout. She finds that her job skills as a full-time production manager for an advertising agency translate easily into quilting. "I really enjoy the chance to design something, produce the whole thing, and come to the final finished product. I like all the different aspects of quilting: I enjoy doing the design; I enjoy picking out the fabric and doing the piecing or appliqué, and then finally the quilting. I just really enjoyed the entire process!" The work was completed over a six-month period, and the artist did admit that the excessive heat of the summer of 1988 made the work difficult and slow going at times. This is the first contest that Maria Forcier has entered.

Me and My Dog Tip by Martha B. Skelton, Vicksburg, Mississippi. 1988. 54½″ x 46½″. Cotton. The artist, who was born in West Virginia and raised in Missouri, has re-created a vision of a happy and untroubled childhood world that recalls the years when she and her five sisters and one brother were free to roam the countryside after attending classes at a one-room schoolhouse. Tip, the dog in the quilt, was her own dog, and she finds that her granddaughter now listens attentively to all the stories she has to tell of her adventures with Tip. Martha Skelton also recalls the fun of making "newspaper kites," and the Popeye cartoon print used in the quilt kite represents many carefree hours of kitemaking and kiteflying during her childhood. A naturalist as well as a professional quilter, the artist traces her love of birds and flowers to her mother, and a number of fond memories of her mother were awakened as she added those images to the quilt. She notes that she had wanted to do a quilt with this theme, and the timing of the contest was "just felicitous." *Me and My Dog Tip* developed its final form from a design in the quilter's head that she realized by cutting out fabric shapes and mounting them on a wall, adding and subtracting until "it was right." Except for the fabric used for the sky and the kite, all the pieces were scraps from other projects. Martha Skelton feels that she makes functional quilts within a traditional style. She is one of a whole family of quilters, including grandmothers, mother, and aunts. She has been quilting since the age of fifteen and teaches quilting now. Many of her quilts have been first prize winners in various contests; most recently in the Mountain Mist International and in some categories of those sponsored by the American Quilters Society in 1986 and 1988. Several of her quilts may be found in the Mountain Mist collection and can also be seen in *Garden of Quilts* by Mary Elizabeth Johnson. She is a member of Jackson Quilters in Jackson, Mississippi, and Big Spur Cotton Patchers in Vicksburg, Mississippi.

Treasures of the Past by Alleta Whittaker, Springfield, Missouri. 1988. 53½″ x 45½″. Cotton, cotton batting. The artist has fond memories of how she and her sister learned their ABCs from "our wonderful aunt and her pretty book," and that book is what supplied the inspiration for this quilt. The appliquéd and embroidered images glow like pieces of stained glass against the dark blue background, and the unusual shape of the quilt adds an extra bit of excitement to the whole. The quilt's basic message is spelled out in a rhyme at its four corners: "Memories of childhood/Days of the past/These are the treasures/That last and last." Each letter block represents something different and special to the maker: "Q" for quilter pictures her own dear grandmother at work; Hiawatha, a favorite childhood story, is the Indian for "I"; Raggedy Ann and Andy at "R" are old favorites; "S" is for seahorses, which she just loves (she notes that the little fish in this block started out as bubbles, but she could not make them round enough, so they became fish instead). "Y" symbolizes her own youth; the child shown represents the young Alleta standing in a field of dandelions that recall the open fields near where she grew up in Chicago and holding the string for the kite, found at "K." Her own children are symbolized by "T" for trains, a major interest and love of her sons. Basically a city girl, Alleta Whittaker found the creation of a chicken ("H" for hen) the most difficult part of the entire quilt! Batting proved to be another difficulty; she tried several types before finding one that would not "beard" through the dark background as she quilted. The idea for an alphabet quilt had been in the artist's mind for some time, and once she had the contest as a goal, the design and execution of the quilt followed readily. Although she has been quilting for six and a half years, this quilt was her first contest entry. It took her eight months to complete, working regularly a few hours a day. The artist is a member of the Ozark Piecemakers Quilt Guild in Springfield.

Packing in Winter Supplies by Sharon Logan, Essex, Montana. 1988. 54″ x 43″. Cotton, polyester batting. Sharon Logan's husband is a national park ranger in Glacier National Park. Every year, as fall comes, the resident park rangers are responsible for resupplying the cabins within the park. These cabins will be the primary refuge for rangers on patrol in the back country during the long winter months, so the responsibility is an important one. Park rangers and their children have carried out this task as a family responsibility through the years, and the quilter's family is no exception. The central medallion in this quilt shows the quilter's husband, their two children, and loaded pack horses ready to bring the winter supplies to the cabins. The faded greens and soft browns and reds represent the colors of autumn and falling leaves, and the glacier that gives the park its name can be seen in the background. The six large pieced Pine Tree squares represent the abundant pine forest found throughout the park, and the path on which the little group is about to embark leads directly into the trees. The quilter said that the most discouraging part of creating this quilt was having to work out for herself a method of appliqué. She had never learned this technique and, as they live in an area that is "almost like a frontier" (only twenty-five people live in Essex), there was no one near at hand to show her how. Sharon Logan started quilting only three years ago, when she decided to make a quilt as a fiftieth-anniversary gift for her parents, and she has already won awards for her work at the Northwest Montana Fair. She finds that she quilts in binges in order to complete a project because their quarters are very tight (a seven hundred-square-foot cabin), and she can't spread her materials out for a long time. Although this places strict limits of time and space on her projects, she enjoys quilting immensely and looks forward to doing many more. With the nearest town sixty miles away and her children's school thirty miles away, she notes that she probably spends more time driving around than quilting!

Picture Books in Winter by Paulette Peters, Elkhorn, Nebraska. 1988. 54¼″ x 45¼″. Cotton. Remember Hiawatha and Cinderella? And Robert Louis Stevenson and Sir Walter Scott and...fairies? An old children's book found in an antiques shop brought all these memories and many more back to Paulette Peters as she worked out the design for this quilt. Peaceful times with books in a snug little area near the blazing fireplace, with light streaming through a window and all the favorite storybook characters waiting to be seen and heard—the artist has captured the essence of those halcyon days of childhood in her depiction of this setting that she says was based on "the room in which I grew up." Robin Hood, Ivanhoe, Snow White, Pinocchio, Heidi, Hans Brinker, Puss 'n' Boots, pirates, and pioneers all find their place in those memories cascading from the shelves in this lively and evocative design. "Picture Books in Winter" is also the title of a poem by Robert Louis Stevenson that begins, "Happy chimney corner days...," an appropriate description of the scene depicted here. Paulette Peters based most of her representations of these storybook characters on pre-1940 illustrations and said that the cascade of figures presented the most technically difficult part of the quilt. In order to achieve exactly the right tone and mood for the quilt, she also found it necessary to hand-dye many of the fabrics to get the proper effect. From concept to completion she spent nearly a year working on the quilt. The artist, who has been quilting since 1975 and was the state winner for the Great American Liberty Quilt Contest in 1986, is a member of four local quilt guilds and has just completed a term as state president for the New England Quilters Guild. She noted that the hardest part of this quilting experience was parting with the quilt itself, but she also found an unexpected side bonus in the project: the search for illustrations and stories for the quilt kindled an interest in old children's storybooks that she is now intent on researching.

Afternoon in the Attic by Bonita K. Hadley, Reno, Nevada. 1988. 54″ x 46″. Cottons, taffeta, wool, silver lamé. The quilt and its title provide a play on words, as the "attic" is both real and symbolic. The physical attic is suggested by the paned window at the left and the vista beyond showing an apple tree and a sky with fluffy clouds. The quilt also alludes to the many memories collected in the "attic" of the quilter's mind, memories that can be taken out and examined any "afternoon" at will. The "Rock-a-Bye Baby" lullaby from a favorite childhood book provided the basic inspiration for this quilt; her mind's "attic" also provided memories of a favorite apple tree, the 1941-style baby dress, and the stars that Bonita Hadley would make wishes on at night. The artist worked from those basics in developing her design; first she methodically listed all the images that she thought she might want to include and then she began to pare away all but those that seemed most important. The final design was carried out through a combination of piecing, appliqué, and embroidery, and the artist included some bits of fabric from her childhood that she had kept through the years. The border quilting echoes the floral appliqués and helps to integrate the overall visual impression created by the design; the flowing ribbon that winds around the border also echoes the curves of the ribbon-edged baby blanket and creates a space in which the baby and her belongings nestle comfortably. It took the artist, who has been sewing since childhood but only recently began quilting, over five hundred hours to complete the quilt; she found that she had to work at least three hours a day in order to be able to complete it by the contest deadline. *Afternoon in the Attic* is her third quilt, but it is the first that she has hand-stitched rather than tied. Bonita Hadley, a professional hairdresser, studied art in college and sees quilting as a "marvelous design medium"; she is a member of the Truckee Meadows Quilters in Reno and is looking forward to much more creative quilting in the future.

Simple Pleasures by Faye Labanaris, Dover, New Hampshire. 1988. 45½″ x 55″. Cottons, Vellex, silver lamé, lace, metallic thread. "The scene in the quilt is the view I see from my window as I sit and quilt. It represents my sons and their pets at play in our yard under a wonderful old apple tree. I see them enjoying the simple and carefree pleasures of childhood and the beauty of nature." The artist has cleverly represented the changing New England seasons as well, from the delicate pink buds of spring through the green leaves and sprinklered garden of summer to the falling leaves of autumn and, finally, to the snows of winter. Her elder son swings merrily in the summer sunshine; her second son thrashes about happily among the autumn leaves; the sledder could be either of the two; the little girl flying a heart-shaped kite in the background of spring may be the artist herself or, perhaps, the daughter she never had. Faye Labanaris notes that "the eleven years since my first son was born have passed as quickly as the four seasons of the year." Her boys were an important element in making the quilt; scraps from their old clothes dressed their figures on the quilt and her older boy sketched out suggestions for parts of the design. "They loved being part of it," the artist says. She also said that she almost didn't enter the contest; the theme intrigued her, but her thoughts about a topic for the quilt remained too vague for a long time. Then she had "a sudden burst of inspiration" and the idea for the changing seasonal scene came to her. She really enjoyed making this quilt, and she finds quilting to be a relaxing and rewarding task. Faye Labanaris is a member of the Cocheco Quilters Guild in Dover, the New England Quilters Guild, and the American Quilters Society; she has been in many shows and won second place in 1987 in a Northfield, Vermont, contest. She started her quilt for this contest in February 1988 with a series of sketches, gathered fabrics through March, and finished her last stitch on August 1. She is already at work designing her next quilt.

Rhymes of My Childhood by Helen B. Andresen, South Plainfield, New Jersey. 1988. 55″ x 45″. Cotton, cotton blends. Some of the most important and delightful childhood memories of the artist center around her first book—a Christmas present of a wonderfully illustrated volume of *Mother Goose* that she still remembers vividly. In this bold, bright, and imaginative quilt she has re-created, through piecing, appliqué, and embroidery, her personal version of many of those old nursery character favorites: Humpty-Dumpty, Jack and Jill, the Old Woman Who Lived in a Shoe, Rock-a-Bye Baby, and the Man in the Moon—to name only a few. A sleepy little girl clutches her own open book of nursery rhymes as she rests against a larger-than-life-size Mother Goose and dreamily visualizes the characters about whom she has been reading. The artist's six-year-old granddaughter posed for the dozing reader as well as for the child in the green raincoat waiting for the rain to stop. Helen Andresen recalls that she considered this volume a most wonderful book; she had many favorites among the nursery rhymes, but she also remembers as a six-year-old her puzzlement about how a dish could run away with a spoon! The artist, who studied at the National Academy of Art and the Art Students League in New York, has been sewing for years; at one point she and a partner had a business making embroidered altar linens for a church in New Jersey. She began quilting only five years ago and came into it as a result of her interest in other fiber arts. The artist entered this contest because she loved the challenge of trying to create the best entry. In making the quilt, she found that she had to redo some parts—particularly the little girl— several times before she was satisfied with the results. She occasionally became discouraged when she had to pull pieces apart, but her enthusiastic and supportive family kept her going and cooperated by helping to make time when she felt that she needed to quilt without interruption for hours at a time.

Greetings by Susan R. Dulaney, Albuquerque, New Mexico. 1988. 55½″ x 46″. Cotton, cotton blends, buttons, polyester batting. Strong light-and-dark contrasts emphasize a highly stylized but amusing design as Susan Dulaney's dogs greet each other among brilliant posies and quilted tulips in the background. The artist achieves another element of clever contrast by stuffing the red flowers until they literally blossom from the quilt ground and by having alternate green leaves float almost free of the quilt surface, thus adding a three-dimensional effect overall. A sure eye developed in a career as a fashion designer has been combined here with memories from earlier years. The artist's father worked for the National Park Service and her childhood was spent in a log cabin (recalled here by the horizontal quilting lines) in the area where he was assigned. Her two pet dogs, one black, the other white, always joined her at play; they are re-created here in sophisticated black-and-white dress prints that make them appear much more elegant than they probably were! The buttons forming the centers of the red flowers remind her of long hours of entertaining herself with boxes of buttons while her older sister was at school; there were no other children nearby with whom she could play. The idea for the design came to her "in a flash" and she completed work on the quilt in only six weeks; the hardest part was deciding on the proper balance of the prints, and careful cutting and piecing give the illusion that each dog is cut from one piece of fabric, which is not the case. Susan Dulaney learned how to sew and to love quilts from her grandmother, who had also been a quilter. When she was about eight years old, her grandmother gave appliqué kits to her and her sister. That first kit took her many years to finish; she was in college by the time it was done! She has been quilting now for about ten years but sees this quilt as being a real turning point for her. She is looking forward to more experimentation with the three-dimensional effect and to designing quilts for interior decor.

Once Upon a Box of Crayons... by Paula Nadelstern, the Bronx, New York. 1988. 46″ x 53½″. Cotton, ultrasuede, cotton blends, found objects. A brilliant and visually exciting quilt that constantly offers new images to the viewer, the design combines sophisticated color abstractions with realistic images. In this quilt, the artist "explores the exciting childhood phenomenon of a brand-new box of crayons; as the escaping colors swirl and tumble, they combine to form kaleidoscopes and other magical images." The new box of crayons may also be said to show the as-yet-to-be-explored potential of childhood. Paula Nadelstern interprets her quilt as follows: "The kaleidoscope piecing used in the quilt represents endless possibilities; the line of Russian babushka dolls shows the child's fascination with infinity; the seahorse represents the beauty and mystery of the ocean; the sun and the moon, the mystery of the universe; and the dragon, childhood fears." The artist knew she wanted to make a quilt with an exciting theme for the contest; she "didn't want fairies" to represent childhood, and the idea of crayons intrigued her and brought back many memories. Once she had decided on the basic theme, she made all the kaleidoscope pieces and then placed them around a more traditional center block. Paula Nadelstern has been quilting for fifteen years and has a wide interest in crafts; she has authored a book, *Quilting Together.* The quilter belongs to no guild, but she has won blue ribbons in the Northern Star Quilt Guild contests of 1983 and 1985 and was also the New York State winner in the Great American Liberty Quilt Contest of 1986. She considers herself to be a professional quiltmaker and has the full support and cooperation of her family when she finds that she needs to devote herself entirely to a project such as this for a very intensive two-month period. As with many of the contest quilters, the artist found that where she went, the quilt went, too, for all of that period!

Down the Dusty Road of Memory by Mary Berry, Hendersonville, North Carolina. 1988. 52½″ x 43″. Cotton, cotton blends, buttons, eyelet, polyester batting. The artist remembers the childhood summers that she spent on her grandparents' farm as being very happy times; she also recalls the quilts that her grandmother had made and felt that this contest provided the right opportunity to create a proper tribute to her. The scene depicted is, of course, her grandparents' farm and other scenes of the area in which they lived. The artist's grandparents sit on the porch of their cozy little house, taking a well-earned rest from daily chores; the general store with its gas pump, the fields, the animals, the barn and other outbuildings are just as the artist sees them in her memory, in family photos, and in her own childhood sketches that she used in developing the design for the quilt. The pigtailed girl looking at the scene, seeing everything "just as she left them," is the artist herself; the fabric of her 1940s-style pinafore recalls the feed-sack dresses that she remembers wearing then. The small quilt hanging on the clothesline copies the design of a quilt that her grandmother had made. The girl's collar and the curtains at the windows are made of eyelet and float slightly free from the quilt, giving a three-dimensional effect to the whole; the border binding changes to match the border fabrics so the eye is not distracted from the central scene. Mary Berry, who started quilting five years ago, is a member of the North Carolina Quilters Guild; she has an honorable mention in a Constitutional Bicentennial contest to her credit, and another of her original designs may be seen in *New Ideas in Lap Quilting* by Georgia Bonesteel. The artist was taking a course in appliqué and had already decided to make a quilt with the farm as its subject when she heard about the contest, so she immediately called upon her newly acquired appliqué skills and, after nine months of patient work, doing a little each day, she produced this very charming and loving look at the past.

Let's Play, Teddy! by Carol A. Lees, Buchanan, North Dakota. 1988. 52″ x 43″. Cotton, polyester batting. A big fabric heart with many little stitched hearts around its edges forms an appropriate background for this charming quilt featuring a happy, smiling teddy bear ready for play with a ball, balloons, and blocks. The hearts are a symbol, perhaps, of the artist's concept of children's thoughts about teddy bears: "They love bears. . . . Teddy bears are among my children's best friends." She readily admits to happy childhood memories of her own teddy bears, and she has certainly seemed to capture the essence of teddy bearness in her interpretation of this plump and perky nursery toy. The artist had actually started a quilt composed of many teddy bears when she heard about the contest, but she ultimately decided that one large happy bear would carry her message best. Carol Lees has also cleverly incorporated more than hearts in the intricate quilting of her design; a sun peeks from behind the clouds in the background, its rays shining down on Teddy, the balloons have festive motifs, and two carefully stitched butterflies decorate his arms and legs. Another subtle detail that helps to add character and charm to the quilt is the use of a contrasting tiny print for the inside of the bear's ear and the bottom of his paw; this same delicate print also forms the small stuffed heart appliquéd on his bottom. The artist, who holds a degree in art, started quilting about ten years ago, when she had her first child. She has made a number of quilts since then, mostly as gifts for friends. She has entered several contests, but this is her first winning quilt, and her success here has encouraged her to plan several more quilt projects. She and her husband own and work a grain and beef farm in North Dakota, and the seasonal nature of their work provides her with the time necessary to devote to quilting. *Let's Play, Teddy!* required five months of work, from the initial idea to completion of the last stitch.

Dress-Up by Beverly L. Melrose, Hinckley, Ohio. 1988. 53½″ x 44½″. Cottons, ultrasuede, buttons, antique beads and tatting. "For all children of all ages, it is fun to play 'dress-up' and 'let's pretend'—it's creative thinking!" So says Beverly Melrose about this imaginative and lively quilt. The three children pictured with piecing, appliqué, and embroidery represent her own, but they could also represent all children who have ever engaged in this favorite pastime, which retains a special appeal that has not dimmed with the years. These children are clearly delighted with their clothing finds, from the tips of their too-big shoes to the top of the boy's well-worn hat complete with resident moth, and they are ready to carry out whatever story line their imaginations and their "dress-up" brings to mind. In addition to the tumble of discarded shoes at the bottom of the quilt, the quilter has cleverly used the reverse side to show a larger collection of appliquéd hats, shoes, and a glove from which the children's final choices undoubtedly were made. The artist decided to enter the contest after seeing an ad for it in a magazine and because she thought "the project would be fun"; she made fourteen designs before deciding that this was the right one. Although the artist remembers her mother quilting, she did not try her hand at it until three years ago, after she retired from twenty-eight years as a high school art teacher. Somehow, between teaching, painting, drawing, and carving decoys, Beverly Melrose had "never found time for it" before! Now, after winning first prize in the Stan Hewett Contest in Akron (the only other contest she has entered) and becoming state winner in this contest, the artist is interested in gaining even greater competence in her new medium as quickly as possible. She is devoting time to attending Quilt Nationals and studying with many of today's foremost quilters; she has, as she says, become delightfully "hooked" on quilts; she has even started to collect old ones, the first of which was a rare find at a garage sale.

Sweet Remembering...Kama'aina Keiki by Mary Alice Kenny-Sinton, Ponca City, Oklahoma. 1988. 54″ x 43″. Cotton. *Kama'aina keiki* means "native-born child" in Hawaiian and represents the son born to Mary Alice Kenny-Sinton twelve years ago in Hawaii. He was five and a half years old when the family left Hawaii, but the scene depicted here—the dramatic landscape of Paradise Park, with its towering peaks, stunning waterfalls, brilliant hibiscus, exotic birds, and lovely waters filled with exciting sealife—will always be part of his childhood memories. The artist has taken a few liberties, but much of the quilt has been executed in the traditional Hawaiian style, where the basic patterns composing the design form mirror images at the right and left. The artist, who has a graphic-arts background, began quilting after she and her mother-in-law became intrigued with Hawaiian quilts; they learned together how to quilt in the Hawaiian style, and they have frequently teamed up to make quilts, usually with Mary Alice Kenny-Sinton designing and her mother-in-law doing the quilting. Their quilts have been pictured in the International Association of Quilters Newsletter and elsewhere. The quilt featured in the newsletter was chosen as one of twenty-one American finalists to be exhibited in Salzburg, Austria. Active in three local quilting groups as well as the Wichita (Kansas) Guild and the British Quilters Guild (her father is British), the artist also teaches needle-turned appliqué for quilts at the local arts center. She calls quilting "my life and work." She had a great deal of fun in working on this project, even to the hand-dying of thirty of the fabrics to add shading and vibrancy to some of the images. She collected ideas and fabrics for the quilt for eight months before actually starting the needlework, and then spent four months working on the quilt itself. She often stays up until midnight or later when she is working on a major project; her husband is happy to do the cooking then, she says, but he insists that she come and eat with him!

Variable Summer Stars by JoAnne Cutler, Corvallis, Oregon. 1988. 53″ x 44″. Cotton, cotton blends. This star-studded quilt designed by JoAnne Cutler captures the memorable summer evenings that she spent sleeping out of doors on the lawn under the clear and starry skies of southern Utah, where she lived as a child. She remembers the red hills and sands of the Western desert, which she felt was reflected in a pinkish glow in the constellations she watched. "The Big Dipper group was the only one I could ever find," she admits. The myriad pink stars scattered on the shaded ground of this quilt is her interpretation of those brilliant nights. The "distorted" stars are original designs, others are adaptations of the traditional star pattern as well as some found in a book of star patterns, *A Constellation for Quilters*, by Carol LaBranche. Another childhood recollection that influences her today is that of her mother and grandmother quilting hundreds of bedcovers, mostly appliqué and whole cloth, to be given to charity (although some went to family members), a Mormon Church tradition; one of their quilts that the artist remembers best was an appliqué quilt made from scraps of her childhood dresses. Today, JoAnne Cutler also pieces quilt tops, including crib quilts, from donated materials for Mormon charities, thus carrying on the tradition. The artist, who is a part-time pharmacist, is basically self-taught and favors contemporary quilts based on traditional designs; she calls herself "an intimidated artist," working in the shadow of her sister, who is a professional artist and a quilter. She has made a number of quilts for family and friends, but this is the first contest she has entered; she decided to enter as a challenge to herself and to see if she could finish in time according to the contest's guidelines. Being the state winner, she says "is one of the biggest thrills of my life. It's really nice to have your work validated by others' opinions." With this encouragement, she hopes to continue her quiltmaking and to compete in more contests in the future.

Connecting Threads by Barbara W. Barber, Westerly, Rhode Island. 1988. 55″ x 44½″. Cotton, satin, velvet, silk brocade, taffeta, satine, silk floss, gold cording. After making over a hundred quilts, Barbara Barber finally created a quilt in honor of the woman who inspired her—her great-grandmother Katie Waite. The artist has shown herself in this quilt as a child sitting at the feet of her paternal ancestor (whom she never knew in real life) and admiring the Crazy quilt in progress, which her great-grandmother made in 1885. That quilt included an embroidered facsimile of a portrait of Queen Victoria, a ribbon from the Washington monument, and Masonic ribbons; one of the artist's childhood memories is having an opportunity to see the quilt as a reward for good behavior! She views "Katie's quilt" as the "connecting thread between generations." In this quilt, she has reproduced the "flavor" of her favorite blocks (including that of Queen Victoria), using them as a frame for the central scene; the gold cording of the border also recalls that of the older quilt. She spent a lot of time thinking about Katie during the three months she worked on the quilt: "It was a learning experience, getting to know her. When I tried to copy her stitches and her colors, it was as if she said, 'I did the best with what I had, now you do your best.' But it felt strange doing the large, dramatic embroidery stitches and putting bitter orange next to mauves and roses." "Katie's quilt" will be passed down to Barbara Barber's brother, but she owns an 1886 sketchbook that her great-grandmother used during one of the summers she spent in Rhode Island. Also a state winner in the Great American Liberty Quilt Contest in 1986, the artist teaches precision quilting and Broderie Perse; her chintz Broderie Perse quilts have received ribbons at the Springfield Fair in Massachusetts (including Best of Show) and at the Vermont Quilt Festival '88. She is a member of the New England Quilters Guild, the Thames River Quilters, and the Narragansett Bay Quilters, and she is cofounder of the Ninigret Quilters.

Rhymes Remembered by Nalda Lagakis, Beaufort, South Carolina. 1988. 54″ x 45″. Glazed cotton chintz, cotton, cotton blends, eyelet, satin. "I'm still a kid at heart," admits the artist, whose nursery-rhyme quilt was inspired by reading the rhymes to her grandson. She also has fond memories of her grandmother and mother reading to her as a child—"a wonderful, innocent time," she recalls. "I hope everyone has the happy memory of their mothers telling these wonderful rhymes." She used a collection of children's books as sources for the rhymes, then designed her own patterns and color combinations, which she noted was the most time-consuming part of making the quilt, albeit satisfying. Each of the twelve appliquéd blocks represents a nursery favorite, from Mother Goose herself through Jack Sprat, Wee Willie Winkle, and Hickory, Dickory, Dock. The appealing blocks are highlighted by a dark floral border adorned with bright little hearts, and more hearts are quilted in both the sashing and border. "I loved making this quilt," says the artist, who spent about two-and-a-half months on the project. "I have so much fun tossing fabrics around!" A self-taught quilter who is originally from New York, Nalda Lagakis began her quiltmaking career in 1953 with kits from a department store, but eventually moved into creating her own compositions. She is not quite sure of the exact number, but knows that she has made over forty quilts, many of which were given to her children and grandchildren, and some of which adorn her own beds and walls; half are bed-size, the rest are wall hangings. Today, she is active designing and making crib quilts for a Charleston toy store. Her good eye for color and design has resulted in a second prize and honorable mention for her crib quilts at the Woodlawn Plantation Quilt Show and a Best in Show award at Oatlands, both in Virginia. Her love of quilts extends to antique textiles, an interest she developed when her mother owned an antiques shop on Long Island, New York. The artist now has a collection of thirty-five old quilts.

For Grandpa by Dawn E. Amos, Rapid City, South Dakota. 1988. 54″ x 45″. *Judge's Choice*. Cotton. Dawn Amos recalls that some of her happiest times as a child were spent on her grandparents' farm in southern Minnesota; there she enjoyed the freedom of "so much room to play" without the restrictions imposed by life in the city. In this poignant memorial quilt for her grandfather, who died in May 1988, she has created a touching visual tribute based on a combination of old photos and memories. "This quilt is for him," the artist says. "I loved him and my memories of the farm." She made the quilt in an intense two months shortly after his death: "After he died, I had to do it to get it out of my system." Surrounding a picture of the young Dawn Amos in the center of the quilt are the farmhouse, her Uncle Merle feeding a lamb, her grandmother's Depression-ware cookie jar (always hidden in the old wood stove), the barn and other farm outbuildings, and a portrait of her grandfather. The "A" represents her grandmother Ada, whom the artist remembers embroidering her initial on all her linens. The artist hand-dyed many of her fabrics in muted browns to produce the subtle and nostalgic sepia effect of old prints. The artist's sister came to visit while she was making this quilt and helped out with laundry, canning, and other household tasks so that she would have the time to finish the quilt before the contest deadline. The two sisters also spent many hours poring over old family photos and reliving happy memories. Dawn Amos was also the state winner in the Great American Liberty Quilt Contest in 1986, her first contest ever; in 1987 and 1988 she was awarded second and third places in the American Quilters Society Professional Appliqué Division. She began quilting ten years ago, influenced by her in-laws, who are Native Americans, and following their tradition she made a number of Star quilts. She now creates and sells quilts of her own design, some of which tell the story of Native American life. She is a member of the Black Hills Quilters Guild.

My World in the 1920s by Mozelle Hendrix, Murfeesboro, Tennessee. 1988. 54¼″ x 45″. Cotton, cotton blends. This nostalgic quilt depicts the rural area around Winston-Salem and the Blue Ridge Mountains where Mozelle Hendrix was born and lived until she was twelve. "My quilt shows houses and buildings as I recall them. Most are no longer standing: the courthouse, my school, the old roller mill, and the row houses are all gone. I can remember riding the twelve miles to town on a dirt road with my father in a Model T Ford....Sometimes we would take an alternate route through Bethabara, a Moravian settlement. The church (built in 1788) and a few Moravian houses are still there." Her grandfather was a tobacco farmer; his house is at top center, with a log tobacco barn to the left. The little house the artist lived in is just below her grandfather's. "Although we were poor, my mother always managed to have curtains at the windows and flowers in the yard." Her father's country store and shop where he repaired cars and farm equipment for fifty years is also included. Mozelle Hendrix says that the quilt gave her "many happy hours of remembering. It had been years since I thought of places like Shore's Dry Goods Store with the big red goose painted on the side, the prettiest thing I'd seen as a child. I could close my eyes and see the familiar curve of the mountains, smell the aroma from the tobacco factory, feel the wind on my face as I played on the swing, see clothes hanging on the line and the round pebbles in Muddy Creek." It also brought back memories of gathering to eat Grandmother's Moravian sugar cakes and big chicken stews. Her one regret is that she couldn't fit everything in! "I am seventy years old and this is the first time I've had the courage to enter any quilt competition," says the artist, whose first effort was a doll quilt when she was nine. Quilting is a family tradition, but her grandmother and mother made quilts for warmth rather than for beauty. The two often coincided, however, and Mozelle Hendrix now prizes a Log Cabin quilt that her mother made.

Treasures by Helen Giddens, Mesquite, Texas. 1988. 45″ x 54″. Cotton, cotton blends. "All the images in this quilt represent some of my strongest youthful recollections," says the artist. "If you look close, you'll see a few in the quilting stitches, too." A tornado passing over her red brick house, her Raggedy Ann doll, a rocket ship, a teddy bear, her favorite chair (that her brother broke), a fanciful armadillo and a colorful rattlesnake, a kite, a TV set, a Mickey Mouse cap, even a bed with a quilt are all fragments of her past included here. She says that the design proved to be the most difficult part; she started with a list of the images she wanted and then had to eliminate—only the TV set and the tornado seemed to remain constant as she went over her list. Helen Giddens, an artist who also paints and makes silk screen prints, has been quilting for fifteen years. She remembers playing under a quilting frame when she was small; her mother made utility quilts, but her grandmother inspired her own creative work with a New York Beauty quilt that she made for the artist's parents. Although she has made traditional quilts for her family, the artist plans to design more contemporary quilts for the future. She has just begun to enter shows and has been named a semifinalist for the 1989 Ohio Quilt National Show. That quilt, which features a southwestern design of armadillos and rattlesnakes, also won third place at the Santa Fe Quilt Festival. Like most quilters, Helen Giddens collects scraps ("fifteen years' worth"), mostly from clothes she has made. Her living room has become a working studio of fabric and butcher paper, and the grasscloth wall is used to measure pieces. As she works full time, she has to make time for quilting when she can. Consequently, she admits that "many things don't get done." Her three children pitch in and help out with the housework to allow her more time for quilting. Despite her flair for creating modern fabric art, the artist says she loves old quilts, enjoys reading about them, and would like to collect them.

Down Hollyhock Lane by Marva Dalebout, St. George, Utah. 1988. 47″ x 55½″. Cotton, cotton blends. "This is probably the most fun quilt I've ever made," says Marva Dalebout, although she admits "sweating blood" designing it; the design changed many times before she was happy with it. The quilt features her childhood playmate Margie and herself in their favorite pastime in rural Utah—spending almost all day playing dress-up in their mothers' dresses and high heels and pushing a doll buggy down a favorite hollyhock-lined lane. Once she started this quilt, she remembers feeling "obsessed" by it; she told everyone about it, and even called her friend Margie to tell her about it, too. Since she retired ten years ago, Marva Dalebout has been "hooked on quilts," taking lessons in Salt Lake City and in California. She began with traditional patterns, but now does her own designs for both patchwork and appliqué. An artist and designer, she has made thirty large quilts and forty wall hangings; most have been gifts for her four children, thirteen grandchildren, and three great-grandchildren. Over the past five years she has taught and conducted workshops in Utah, Nevada, and California and has been featured in many quilt exhibits and magazines. She won second place in the master's category at the Utah Quilt Guild, of which she is a member, and fourth place in the 1987 *Better Homes & Gardens* Small Quilt Contest. Her enthusiasm for bright colors and unusual prints is evident in this quilt, and she will hand-dye fabrics if she cannot find just the effect she is looking for. Before she begins a quilt, the artist paints a watercolor of it using the colors she plans to use; she also photographs and marks each creation with her name and the date. She does most of her quilting with a fourteen-inch hoop, because she can take it with her on her travels or even from room to room. "I can't think of anything nicer than to leave something like this, made with love and care, for future generations," says Marva Dalebout.

Through McGregor's Garden by Jodi G. Warner, Salt Lake City, Utah. 1988. 54½" x 44½". Cotton. *Judge's Choice*. This delightful and colorful quilt is a "fantasy celebration of *Peter Rabbit* in three-dimensional detail. It was designed to bring the story to life for children as well as to recall childhood memories," says the quilter. From top to bottom of the quilt, she retells Peter's adventures in the familiar Beatrix Potter tale in a creative way that encourages the viewer to touch and feel, to become involved. Some fabric pieces, such as the rabbits' ears, the watering-can handle, the jackets, and the pinafore aprons, have been left loose or only partially stitched to the background; fluffy cottontails and padded-and-folded cabbages further enhance the three-dimensional effect. The intricate stitching throughout adds to the textural sense of the piece, and the frisky rabbits running around the border help to emphasize the theme. Jodi Warner's inspiration for this lively creation came from reading the story to her two young children and from her fond remembrances of the lovely illustrations. Once she had decided on her theme, she found it "so exciting, it was hard to settle down and not jump in without completing the design first!" She became so involved in the quilt that she put her business interests aside until it was completed. A professional quilt designer who was trained in fashion design, the artist now markets her own patterns through her company, Hearthsewn, and teaches quilting at local shops. She is a member of the Utah Quilt Guild and was awarded Best of Show in a Utah quilt show a few years ago. That award brought an invitation to her and to several other Utah quilters to compete in a California show, from which they returned with a new collection of awards. Jodi Warner grew up in the Mormon pioneer tradition; she recalls quilts made and recycled by her grandmother and her mother, who encouraged her to sew. As a teenager, she took adult education quilting classes and now, thirty quilts later, still finds quiltmaking a joy and delight.

Hail to the Prince by Mary P. Kennedy, Brandon, Vermont. 1988. 54″ x 46½″. Cotton, cotton blends, polyester. When Mary Kennedy was finishing her medieval fairy-tale quilt, she discovered that it was seven inches too narrow to meet the contest guidelines! No problem, however—she just added a tower on each side, which not only fitted the design but added the necessary extra inches! In a scene reminiscent of the books "my father used to read to us and the neighbor children when we lived in Albany, New York" (and that she also read to her grandchildren), her appliquéd scrap quilt pictures a baby prince being brought to church for christening, amid great celebration, by the ladies-in-waiting. Her design is not based on any specific story but rather is intended to capture the flavor of the lovely illustrations the artist remembers accompanying the stories. The most distinctive feature in her work is the texture quilting; in this quilt, she achieved an unusual tactile quality by using stitching rather than piecing to shape the clouds, the building masonry, and the paving stones. A watercolorist with an art degree, Mary Kennedy taught for eighteen years in Vermont schools before retiring six years ago. Since then, she has been doing embroidery and crewel, rug-hooking, knitting, and smocking in addition to quilting. Most of her needlework is done while watching TV at night. The artist took up quilting after her retirement, and she recalls that in 1870, her great-grandmother won first prize for her quilt at the New York State Fair. The artist has now made about twenty quilts, including some put together from antique blocks (a few of which date from the Civil War) that her brother found and one done in Hawaiian style. When she visited her daughter in Hawaii, she became fascinated by the quilts there, and so she decided to make one for her daughter. Mary Kennedy spent two months working on the quilt for this contest and notes, "I get a big charge out of quilting when a project takes off on its own!"

Patches of Memories in the Maze of Childhood by Linda M. Pool, Vienna, Virginia. 1988. 55″ x 46″. Cotton, ultrasuede, synthetics, mink, metal, rubber, paper, feathers, wood, plastic, hair, string, assorted other items. *Imaginative Use of Detail Award.* Linda Pool has captured myriad childhood memories in this lively quilt; the children depicted represent her own family, but the patchwork maze of the nostalgic events that she has portrayed belong to all children. The pathways lead the youngsters through many experiences, until "they grow up with lasting memories," according to the artist. She has filled her quilt with familiar and joyful images: the holidays and presents, visiting the zoo, storytime, warm cookies right from the oven, pets, picnics, favorite toys and games, and fishing—to name a few. Some scenes have a special personal meaning, such as playing dress-up, swinging on her country swing, and saying nightly prayers; "Since I came from a Mennonite family, prayer played a big part in my life," she notes. One scene, that the artist calls "In Disgrace," shows a little girl standing in a corner and being consoled by her dog; it is a reminder that childhood isn't always fun and games! The artist, who is also a miniatures collector, added many tiny objects to give her work a dimensional feel: Christmas tree ornaments, a framed picture, a pocket watch for the balloon man, a tire swing, metal fish, a wooden slingshot are all included. She made an ultrasuede teddy bear and a braided rug to attach to the quilt. Pieces of string, toothpicks, and real hair also found their way into the quilt. While making the quilt, the artist was having two house additions built and did her husband's business bookkeeping. "Although it was difficult to make, it was fun and kept me sane during a hectic period," she says. A quilter for about twelve years, Linda Pool was inspired by her Pennsylvania grandmother, who quilted all her life. She belongs to Quilters Unlimited in northern Virginia, and her work has brought her five ribbons at Woodlawn Plantation's Needlework Show.

Missouri Memory by Shirley Perryman, Pullman, Washington. 1988. 53½″ x 43½″. Cotton. "The central design represents my grandparents' farm as I remember it. I spent almost every weekend there until I was nine years old. My grandfather milked the cows morning and night, and I was usually there to help get the cows in. As children, we played in the barn, and I remember that my grandmother had a white cat. My grandmother tended the garden behind the house, and she was the one who taught me how to sew. The checkerboard border, the only repetitive part of the quilt, represents games we played as children." All these memories and more are represented in this quilt, the first pictorial one that Shirley Perryman has made. This became a very special quilt to her during the three months she worked on it: "I became more consumed by this quilt than by any other that I have made." She remembers a vacation trip to Seattle that she spent quilting throughout the five-hour car ride there and back! She is thrilled to have been selected as winner for her state, and the honor has fired her to continue quilting. Although Shirley Perryman has been sewing since childhood, she only made her first quilt in 1986; since then, she has been a finalist in the *Quilter's Newsletter Magazine* Big 200 Contest and second place winner in the Quilt Nebraska Contest, both in 1988. The artist composes her designs on a special flannel wall in her studio; after cutting out the pieces, she sticks them on the wall (just like a child's flannel storyboard) and moves them around or trims them until the design fits and works. She felt that the hardest part of making this quilt was working out the dimensions of the buildings; the henhouse is, perhaps, larger than it should be, but that is the way it looms in her memory: "One of my jobs was to collect the eggs in the chicken house. I hated collecting the eggs! The chickens would peck at me, and I used to take a broom to hold them back until I could get the eggs from the nests. My grandmother never knew what I went through to get those eggs!"

Chasing Fireflies by Janet Underwood, Franklin, West Virginia. 1988. 53″ x 43″. Cotton, cotton/polyester blends. "I remember when fireflies seemed like stars come to earth. I loved fireflies when I was a child....I used to chase them and put them in bottles to save them." These memories, along with the immediate environment of the West Virginia mountains in the glowing evenings of summer, prompted the design for this quilt that sparkles with stars and fireflies. The artist's fine-arts background and training in oil painting is evident in the swirl and flow of fabric in land and sky. Janet Underwood has been quilting for sixteen years, and this is her smallest quilt in ten, as she prefers to work in larger formats both in quilts and in paint. She is a three-time participant in the Vandalia, West Virginia, Annual Quilt Show; she has also won honorable mention in a manufacturer's contest that required the use of one of the manufacturer's patterns but allowed free rein in the use of color and fabric. "Color selection is my favorite part of quilting; I don't consider myself a great technician—I'm in quilting for the sense of color, of design, of movement. Other than the border, there are few straight pieces in this quilt, and that adds to the sense of movement." The artist noted that she had some reservations about the quilt and would do some parts differently if she could do it over. "I felt that as a baby quilt, it shouldn't be too dark, yet it is a night scene and I think that parts got too light. I found it difficult to balance the needs between a night scene and a quilt suitable for a crib." The most difficult part of entering the contest centered around submitting the slides of the quilt; the slides were taken at the last minute and the photo processor did not return them on schedule. Since she and her husband were about to leave for New Mexico to take their son to college and would not return until after the deadline for submission, she had to leave to a friend the task of choosing and sending the slides. She has yet to see the slides that brought her into the finalists' circle!

Designing Doll Dresses by Jean Teal, Oconomowoc, Wisconsin. 1988. 55½" x 44½". Cotton, laces, buttons. The artist purchased the fabrics used in this quilt at an auction in 1976 and had been waiting ever since for the right occasion to use them. She recalls that there were over a hundred quarter-yard pieces of old fabrics, mostly dating from the 1930s and 1940s, in a big wooden box. The box sat in her attic for years, but when she designed the twenty-five blocks for this quilt, she knew she had found the perfect use for them. Jean Teal has been sewing since she was eight years old, and she always wanted to be a dress designer (as does her sixteen-year-old daughter today). When she was eleven, she received a Toni doll (one with hair that could be washed, set, and curled) for Christmas and immediately started making dresses for it. Her twenty-five-cent allowance, she remembers, was almost always spent on fabric that she used to make dresses for her doll. Although the artist spent several months trying and discarding designs for the quilt, she finally realized that because the doll had figured so largely in her childhood and had so strongly influenced her activities, it was the only right theme to use—and she still has that doll today. Once started, the quilt totally consumed Jean Teal for three months; it seemed that everywhere she went and everything she did somehow related to the quilt, and she recalls her daughter telling her that she "wasn't too nice all summer." The artist looked at old sewing patterns and old issues of *Life* magazine to come up with authentic styles from the 1930s and 1940s, and many of the blocks remind her of dresses her mother wore. Most people, she notes, prefer the two 1940s tunic-style dresses with black skirts, but her favorite is the 1930s-style pink dress (second from the right in the third row). Although the quilter has made more than twenty-five machine-stitched quilts (mostly for sale), this is the first that she has hand-stitched, as well as the first contest she has entered. She is a member of Wisconsin Quilters Inc.

Spring on the Farm by Sarah May Robinson, Cheyenne, Wyoming. 1988. 53″ x 43″. Cotton, cotton blends. Inspiration for this quilt came from memories of a childhood spent on a farm, where the eight cows were milked by hand. The design, which is executed with appliqué and some embroidery, proved a problem only in the number of things that could be shown. The artist said that there were so many scenes of life on the farm that she had wanted to include, but when she laid out all the pieces there was just too much to fit in the space available and so it was necessary to start taking away in order to find just the right balance for the size of the quilt. The farm scenes are made from remnants left over from other quilts made by the artist, and she said she had some difficulty in finding just the right scraps of fabric to give her the colors she wanted with which to produce the lively design. Sarah May Robinson, married for forty-six years, started quilting shortly after her marriage "just for fun" and hasn't stopped since; she said that when she showed her first completed quilt to an aunt, she was told, "You darned it, not quilted it!" Her husband made wooden toys in the evenings while she would "set and quilt"; it was her way of making artwork to be used and enjoyed. She has no idea of the number of quilts that she has made over the years, but there have been at least thirty or forty. A few were made for sale, but most were made for family and friends. She notes that her family loves her quilts, and her three sons say they "won't sleep under anything else!" Another quilt created by Sarah May Robinson won second prize at the county fair this year, but this is the first national contest she has entered. The contest was brought to her attention only two months before the deadline by a home health-care nurse who was attending her mother. Once the artist decided to enter the contest, she spent nearly every waking moment working on the quilt, "stopping only long enough to eat!" The nurse was promised a steak dinner should Sara May Robinson be a contest winner.

I Broke the Gander's Leg by Denise Vanderlugt, Proserpine, Queensland, Australia. 1988. 53½″ x 45½″. Cotton, polyester, cotton blends. *Judge's Choice*. The artist's family was concerned when she told them that she would be doing a quilt based on her childhood memories; they worried that going over the past would cause her to relive the hard times that they had once experienced when living in Rockhampton, Australia. When the completed quilt was displayed, however, everyone was delighted, both with the concept and execution. The memories Denise Vanderlugt chose to depict give a reflection of how attuned to nature she is and how much pleasure it gave her even when she was a small child. The design shows the gray geese that were used as "watchdogs" on her family's poultry farm. She remembers that "the old gander would always attack us children. To make him leave me alone, I would grab him by the neck and throw him away. One day, he landed incorrectly and broke his leg. I had to catch him, put on a splint, and bandage that leg. My dad helped me to do this." The artist also notes that a piece of fabric in the quilt is actually a scrap from one of her mother's dresses. But there is much more to the quilt than a childhood memory: "The brown colors are reminiscent of the dry climate and yearly fires in that area of Australia. The blue water reflects the brilliant Australian skies." Today, the artist lives in a lusher area of the country, and she and her husband are in the midst of planting tropical rain-forest vegetation that they hope will attract butterflies. She has made other quilts that convey the qualities of this area, where the colors are very bright; but no matter what part of Australia is portrayed, her goal remains the same: to spur efforts at conservation. The artist hopes that her work will encourage the viewer to become more aware of one's natural surroundings and to "look at life in a new way." A full-time quilter, she has exhibited extensively; one of her quilts traveled throughout Australia as part of the Quilt Australia '88 Traveling Suitcase exhibition.

Memories Playground by Sheila Ruth Mahoney, Zephyr, Ontario, Canada. 1988. 52½″ x 43″. Chiffon, satin, linen, wool, cotton, brocade, ribbon, velvet. Every scrap of the many fabrics in this quilt represents a specific memory and originally belonged to the quilter, members of her family, or friends; they had all been saved over the years in anticipation of finding just the right use for them someday. The lively design depicts the important people (both adults and children), events, and scenes of the artist's childhood, which she describes as being very "rich in people and experiences." Her family roots are represented by a "field of sunny yellow linen from Ireland, the warm woolen batting from Scotland, and the sky-blue linsey-woolsey backing from England (dyed here at home to get just the right shade)." The many circles scattered over the quilt represent all the balls, yoyos, balloons, pucks, cookies, suns, and moons of childhood; cats, dogs, birds, and fish may be reminders of family pets; posies and toys bring other memories to the fore. All the action joyously whirls around the anchors of childhood: the rose-colored cottage that symbolizes home, the white-steepled church with stained-glass windows, the old red schoolhouse where many hours were spent. "The earthy browns of the border form a fence, always around the grounds we played in, like a big hug, keeping us safe, and today, enfolding those precious childhood memories." Sheila Ruth Mahoney is a self-taught artist; she describes herself as "a person who makes things." She spins, weaves, hooks rugs, sews, and paints in addition to quilting. People who visited her at her small farm began to commission her to make pieces for their own use, and word of mouth has brought even more—she is constantly amazed at the number of people who find their way to her doorstep! She is especially proud of the fact that her hand-hooked rugs are in the collection of the National Museum of Civilization in Ottawa.

Blow the Winds Southerly by Linda Negandhi, Iffley, Oxford, England. 1988. 53″ x 45½″. *Workmanship Award*. Liberty Tana lawn. "I grew up by the sea at Gosport, between Portsmouth and Southampton. I used to watch the boats on the Solent, and I loved to see their spinnakers unfurled," this artist says of her childhood. "The sea was a big part of our lives; I remember spending every waking moment walking on the beach, sailing, finding cuttlefish. Making this quilt brought back many memories." The quilt was created using the English piecing method, in which each cloth shape is first sewn over a paper template before the pieces are joined together with whip stitches. The artist designed her quilt full size on paper and used that design to create her templates. The exceptionally detailed quilting highlights her strong graphic presentation and carries through the theme of the sea in the shells, anchors, and seahorses that appear in the stitching on the white border. The interior blue-and-white border represents nautical rope, and the navy-and-pale-blue outer border symbolizes speed. The artist, who spent nearly five months making the quilt, found that she needed to hand-dye many of the pieces herself to achieve the gradations of color she wished for the sea and for the brilliant, jewel-like tones of the sails. Both her grandmother and her mother were skilled needlewomen, and Linda Negandhi learned the basics of quilting from her mother; she has been quilting now for about two years. Her zest for quilting started with a 1981 London exhibition of modern and traditional quilts; she found that the block patterns excited her interest and sense of design. Members of a Women's Institute in Iffley that she had joined then encouraged her to attempt a full-size quilt on her own, and it was subsequently entered in a national exhibition in 1987. As England lacks the broad network of quilt guilds found in the United States, and the nearest group is far from where she lives, the artist notes that she is often very much "on her own" as she continues to design, piece, and quilt.

Le Cirque by Denyse Saint-Arroman, Toulouse, France. 1988. 54½″ x 45″. Cotton, cotton blends, silk, satin. "When I was a child, life was rather dull without TV and few movies. So, a circus arrival in town was a big event, to be remembered for a long time," recalls the maker of this gay circus scene. Denyse Saint-Arroman was the daughter of a French military officer and lived in many areas of France when she was a child: "The circus traveled through all the villages, and it was wonderful." She based her design for the circus grounds and tents on popular French picture books and the parade of animals, acrobats, and clowns prancing around the border were based on a Walt Disney film. A fabric collector, she selected French and American textiles and bands of Liberty prints for the quilt. A piece of antique lace of her grandmother's also found its way into the work, and the petit-point edging enhances the provincial look the artist hoped to achieve. Denyse Saint-Arroman learned hand embroidery at the age of five and did tapestry work in her early years in France, but it was ten years ago, while living in Ft. Sill, Oklahoma, where her French Army officer husband was stationed, that she joined a quilting group and learned to quilt—it was a good way to make friends, she says. Now back in France, the artist is a member of the Association Français de Patchwork; she writes for their newsletter and has organized a local quilt group. As quilting books are difficult to obtain in France, she says she subscribes to American quilt magazines and buys a "fortune's worth" of books and fabrics when she visits her daughter in England. She has completed seventeen quilts, which she has sold or given to friends. She often quilts eight hours a day, making pieced and Broderie Perse quilts, one of which received third prize in a French contest, in addition to appliqué pieces. Once started on a quilt, the artist likes the sense that "it grows by itself"; quilting presents no difficulty to her, but she finds the design takes the most time "to give the feeling that you want."

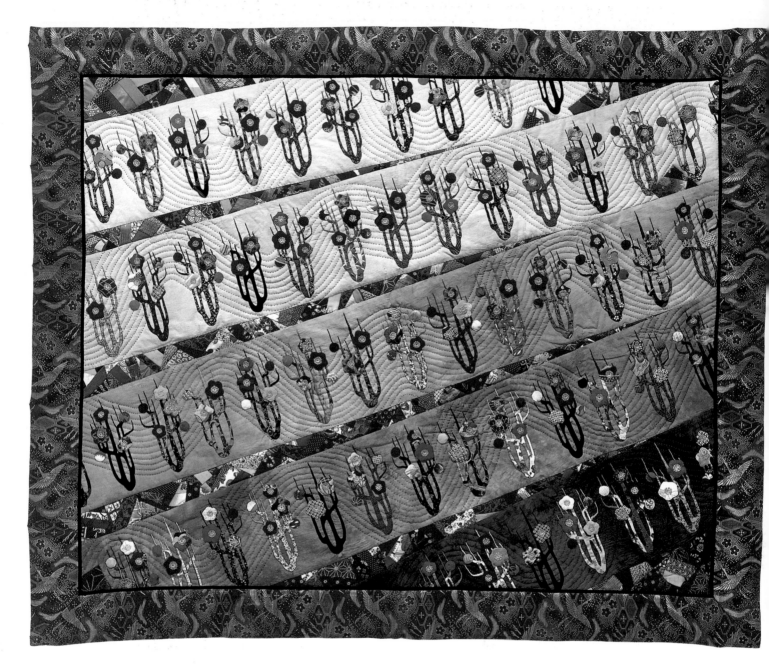

Haru O Matsu (Waiting for Spring) by Sanae Hattori, Yokohama, Japan. 1988. 45″ x 54″. Cotton, silk, polyester. The weeping plum blossoms represented in this quilt actually bloom in January, so they are the first indication that the end of winter is near. When the blossoms appear (and no leaves appear until after the petals fall), it is the cue to begin the preparations for Girls' Day festival, a holiday of major importance for young Japanese girls up to the age of ten. Although the festival does not take place until March 3, it is customary to set up the elaborate decorations for it—a display of tiered steps with prince and princess dolls and all their royal attendants and equipment—well ahead of time. Girls look forward to the festival with great excitement, and the displayed dolls are a reminder of all they will enjoy that day, such as wearing a special kimono and visiting their temple and families and friends. Sanae Hattori wanted to convey this sense of waiting and anticipation in the imagery in this brilliant quilt; she also included strong diagonal slashes of brightly colored patchwork intended to represent the *chiyogami,* or "gaily colored paper," that young girls use for paper-folding and games. The artist, who has been a master of traditional Japanese embroidery for over twenty years, was first introduced to American quilts through an exhibition in Japan fifteen years ago. At that time, "there were no books or magazines, no teachers, and no materials"; thus, she taught herself by looking at pictures, by trial and error, and by research in American magazines—when she could find them. She is now considered a master quilter, has published books on quilting, and has her own school. She notes that creating the design was fun, but "the most difficult part was the appliqué technique for all those little plum blossoms! And it took a long time to find just the right piece of fabric for the border. I was beginning to think that I would run out of time, then I discovered just what I was looking for—the perfect color in an antique *obi* sash for a kimono that I found at a flea market. I was quite relieved!"

Grandfather Took Me to the Zoo to See the Elephants by Jo Cornwall, TePuke, New Zealand. 1988. 54½″ x 45″. Cotton, polyester batting. "I will always remember grandfather taking us to the zoo," Jo Cornwall says. This quilt is, in essence, a tribute to her grandfather, who became something of a father substitute because her own father was crippled and could not do much with the children. She notes that making the quilt brought back many memories of her grandfather and what he had meant to her when she was a child. She also remembers being impressed by the elephants at the zoo, and she has clearly caught a sense of their movements and personalities in this colorful piece. She designed her quilt full size and then cut it up to guide cutting the pieces. The Crazy-quilt effect was planned as part of the design, and the striped border helps to "contain" the design much as the zoo fence contains the elephants! She deliberately kept the quilting simple so that the design would be dominant and thus the embroidered and appliqué elephants would take center stage. Jo Cornwall is from a long line of "domestic artists," but there is no tradition of quilting in New Zealand. She learned quiltmaking on her own, with the help of a book, as a matter of necessity—she needed a quilt and couldn't afford one. She has now made a number of quilts in the ten years since that first one; she has won several quilt contests in New Zealand and exhibits and sells in galleries as well. She did not complete school as a young woman, but at age forty she started night school to complete her education. She has studied painting and design and hopes to go on to further study at an art school; right now, she considers quilting her job. The artist said that *Grandfather Took Me to the Zoo to See the Elephants* took her just one month to complete, working full time on it. Although she was convinced that the project was worth doing, she admits to getting discouraged halfway through; she put the quilt away for a few days and was then able to return and finish it with renewed spirit.

Happy Days by Anne M. Chenaux, Blonay, Switzerland. 1988. 53″ x 44½″. Cotton, satin, polyester, polyester batting. Delightful animal favorites cavort in the blocks of this quilt, each telling its own story of a specific activity or event related to the months and seasons of the year. A turtle finds a sporty use for his shell in January; a fox skates with aplomb in February; a sleepy skunk greets the receding snows of March; a bunny, Easter egg, daffodil, and baby chick usher in April; lively songbirds sing a chorus to May; an insect orchestra plays a lively tune for dancing ladybugs in June; an elephant frolicks in the water on a sultry July day; mice come out for play in the freshly mown fields of August; a squirrel harvests its winter stores in September; a frog sits out a tempestuous October storm; an owl, a pumpkin, and a crescent moon symbolize November; and Santa Claus, with a merry "Ho, Ho, Ho!" closes the year of this charming quilt calendar. Stitching was used to give special additional meaning to a scene, and the satin used in the winter scenes represents the glow and shimmer of ice and snow. Anne Chenaux notes that she used extra-thick batting in this quilt because "nights are cold in Switzerland!" The design was her own inspiration, based on memories of her childhood activities throughout the year. Coming up with the design, she says, "was the most difficult part of the quilt, and I wondered if I could do it, but I never got discouraged." She felt the theme of the contest provided a "real challenge," and that is why she entered. The artist started quilting in 1984 and taught herself by reading books. This is the fifth quilt that she has made; she spent "a bit more than 250 hours working on it, over three and a half months, after the design was finished," and she even took it with her during the holidays. She finds that she cannot work a little every day on quilting: "When I do quilting, it is for many hours; I usually do it at night, until two or three in the morning." She became a member of Patchwork of Leman in 1987 to "find out what others were doing in patchwork."

Animal Puzzle by Inge Schulz-Loffler, Leopoldshohe, West Germany. 1988. 53″ x 45½″. Cotton. *Animal Puzzle* is a wonderful quilted and appliquéd exercise in search and discover. Can you find a kangaroo? A dog? A chicken? A crocodile? A squirrel? A mouse? A duck? A partridge? They are all here, as well as fish, a cockatoo, a shark, a rabbit, a frog, a penguin, a bear, a camel, and a zebra! This quilt with two surfaces was created as a riddle for children; the idea first came to the artist when her eleven-year-old son was hospitalized for many months and she spent hours playing games and doing puzzles with him. Her son is now well, and the completed quilt is a delight for all the children who see it as they learn to find and name the seventeen animals incorporated in the design. The colors were purposely limited to red, black, and white, and the animals were formed from positive and negative versions of a sprightly Westphalian print; one small motif from two versions of the print forms the eyes of the animals, thus giving clues to help in finding them. The contrasting print is used as the overlap for each animal, another aid to identification. Quilting on the appliquéd animals and on the border has been kept to a minimum, but point stitches carefully dot the background cloth and give texture to the whole as well as provide strong delineation for the animal forms. The artist made her first quilt eight years ago; it was a Grandmother's Flower Garden pattern and she was astonished to see pieces quite similar to hers at an exhibit because she had never seen the pattern before making her quilt. Her mother-in-law, a Mennonite, had learned to quilt while living in South America in 1953; she needed to make blankets for warmth, and sometimes scraps of fabric were all that was available. This intrepid lady served as a source of inspiration for the artist. Inge Schulz-Loffler, a teacher and accomplished seamstress, would someday love to quilt for a living. She has been widely exhibited in Europe and Japan and is a member of the Patchwork Gilde of North Germany.

SEMIFINALISTS IN THE MEMORIES OF CHILDHOOD CONTEST

Alabama: Linda Waselkov
Alaska: Raenell Doyle
Arizona: Shirley Murdock
Arkansas: Patricia Eaton
California: Janet L. Paluch
            Sachiko Sudo
Colorado: Sherri Driver
Connecticut: Barbara C. Harris
Delaware: Nancy Stanford Davis
District of Columbia: Neisja Yenawine
Florida: Peggy A. Horsfield
Georgia: Marion Rowen
Hawaii: Stanley Yates
Idaho: Jane Frazier
Illinois: Suesi Metcalf
         JoAnne Hemmer Sapadin
Indiana: Christine Deitchley
Iowa: Virginia M. Wing
Kansas: Suzanne Warren Brown
Kentucky: Rebekka Seigel
Louisiana: Patricia Kruelski
Maine: Shirley Boulanger
Maryland: Kathy Hardis Fraeman
Massachusetts: Nancy Prendergast
Michigan: Elsie Vredenburg
Minnesota: Julie K. Miscera
Mississippi: Ollie May Grant
Missouri: Suzanne Marshall
Montana: Marcia June Wilson
Nebraska: Shelley Burge
Nevada: Mary Thomson
New Hampshire: Lucinda McKenney

New Jersey: Judy B. Dales
New Mexico: Deborah S. Sarabia
New York: Patricia Mink
North Carolina: Julia Spidell
North Dakota: Mrs. Carl Erie
Ohio: Gale Thomson
      Susan G. Hargrave
Oklahoma: Mary Helen Ritan
Oregon: Dorothy Herberg
Pennsylvania: B.J. Elvgren
Rhode Island: Gayle White Antunes
South Carolina: Susan Bates
South Dakota: Shirley C. Fresquez
Tennessee: Rosann Wood
Texas: Mary Ann Herndon
Utah: Laura Tomita Lyons
Vermont: Suzanne Schoolcraft
Virginia: Michele Vernon
Washington: Stephanie Lee Ostman
West Virginia: Eileen Squitiro
Wisconsin: Rita Menet
Wyoming: Cynthia A. Curtright
Australia: Yolanda M. Gifford
Canada: Faye S. Steckley
France: Françoise Leroy Garioud
Japan: Noriko Isshiki
The Netherlands: Liesbeth Spaans-Prins
Sweden: Mari-Ann Castenvik
Switzerland: Claudine Joho
United Arab Emirates: Christine Manzo
West Germany: Natacha Wolters